D1286957

THE COUNTRYMAN'S BRITAIN

CONTRIBUTORS

Tristram Beresford
David St John Thomas
Gerald Wibberley
Ronald Blythe
Charles Arnold-Baker
Reg Hookway
George Ryle
Victor Bonham-Carter
Bruce Campbell
Christopher Hall
Tony Aldous
Crispin Gill

THE
COUNTRYMAN'S
BRITAIN

Edited by
CRISPIN GILL

DAVID & CHARLES
NEWTON ABBOT   LONDON
NORTH POMFRET (VT)   VANCOUVER

ISBN 0 7153 7284 X
Library of Congress Catalog Card Number 76-21022

Set in 12 on 13pt Bembo
and printed in Great Britain
by Latimer Trend & Company Ltd Plymouth
For David & Charles (Publishers) Limited
Brunel House   Newton Abbot   Devon

Published in the United States of America
by David & Charles Inc
North Pomfret   Vermont 05053   USA

Published in Canada
by Douglas David & Charles Limited
1875 Welch Street   North Vancouver BC

CONTENTS

LIST OF ILLUSTRATIONS

THE CONTRIBUTORS

Tristram Beresford received degrees from Oxford and Cambridge Universities, and the CBE for services to agriculture in 1966. For twenty-five years he and his partners were tenant farmers on a 900-acre chalkland farm on Salisbury Plain. Tristram Beresford has been involved in most areas of agriculture, including arable farming in England and hill farming in Wales and Scotland. He writes regularly for *The Countryman* and was agriculture correspondent of the *Financial Times* for fourteen years. He also lectures in France, on Britain in Europe, for the Foreign and Commonwealth Office. He is the immediate past-president of the Agricultural Economics Society and is now on the Management Council of Oxfam. His first publication, *Break of Day*, was published in 1937.

David St John Thomas began his career as a journalist, became a railway expert and developed a strong interest in the country; he founded David & Charles as a hobby and is now chairman of the David & Charles group of companies. He is author of about a dozen books and is currently producing *The Country Railway*.

Dr Gerald Wibberley, Ernest Cook Professor of Countryside Planning in the University of London and Vice-Principal of Wye College, the agricultural faculty of London University, went from his grammar school at Abergavenny to the universities of Wales, Oxford and Illinois, USA. After service with war agricultural committees and then

9

the Ministry of Agriculture, where he built up a team studying agricultural aspects of town and country planning, he moved to Wye College in 1954 as head of the Department of Economics. He became Professor of Rural Economy in 1963 and the first holder of the Ernest Cook chair, held jointly between Wye College and University College, London, in 1969. He was awarded the CBE for services to countryside planning in 1972 and is President of the Agricultural Economics Society 1975-6.

Ronald Blythe's family has been associated with Suffolk for many generations and he has lived there all his life. He became a full-time writer in 1955. His books include *A Treasonable Growth* (novel), *Immediate Possession* (short stories), *The Age of Illusion* (history), and *Akenfield*; critical writing includes studies of Jane Austen, William Hazlitt and Thomas Hardy. He has also written a number of films, amongst which are *A Painter in the Country* (John Nash), *Constable Observed*, both BBC TV, and *Akenfield*, Peter Hall's cinema version of some of the themes belonging to the book. He has been a contributor to *The Countryman* since 1957.

Charles Arnold-Baker was born in Berlin in 1918 and educated at Winchester, Oxford, and in the army; called to the bar in 1948, he practised mostly in Admiralty until becoming Secretary of the National Association of Parish Councils (now Local Councils). He was a member of the Royal Commission on Common Lands, and has written books on Parish and Community Councils and Local Government Law as well as a short work called *The 5000* on the British Constitution. He has nearly finished the *Oxford Companion to British History*, is more or less trilingual and 'sometime or other I collected a minor Norwegian decoration and an OBE'.

Reg Hookway went to the grammar school in his native Bideford and on to the then University College of the South-West at Exeter. He returned there after war service, and in 1948 joined the infant planning department of Devon County Council. In 1958 he was appointed deputy county planning officer with the Norfolk County Council. He joined the National Parks Commission in 1965 as Principal Planning Officer, before going to the Ministry of Housing & Local Government in 1969 as Deputy Chief Planning Officer. He returned to the Countryside Commission as Director in 1971.

George Ryle, after reading forestry under professors Schlich and Troup in the old School of Forestry at Oxford, joined the Forestry Commission in October 1924 as a District Officer on probation. Apart from being seconded for timber production duties during the war, he remained with the Commission until he retired exactly 41 years later. After the war he became successively Director of Forestry for Wales, Director of Forestry for England and finally Deputy Director General. After retirement to Bank, near Lyndhurst, he was appointed a Verderer of the New Forest. He is a Fellow and medallist of the Institute of Foresters of Great Britain. He was created CBE in 1960.

Victor Bonham-Carter farmed in west Somerset after the war and served on Exmoor National Park committees. He is now President of the Exmoor Society and lives near Dulverton. He has written a number of books on farming and country life, notably *The Survival of the English Countryside* (Hodder 1971). He helps to run the Exmoor Press, publishing authoritative monographs about the wildlife and history of the moor. Married, with two sons and six grandchildren, he works in London during the week as Joint Secretary of the Society of Authors and Secretary of the Royal Literary Fund.

Bruce Campbell trained as a forester, spent some years in education and eventually emerged, by way of a PhD on bird populations, ten years as Secretary of the British Trust for Ornithology and three as head of the BBC's Natural History Unit, as *The Countryman*'s editorial adviser on natural history and wildlife conservation. He was created OBE in the 1976 New Year Honours List.

Christopher Hall has been Director of the Council for The Preservation of Rural England since 1974 and was national Secretary of the Ramblers'

Association 1969–74. He founded the Chiltern Society and served as its honorary secretary 1965–8, and he has been involved at committee level with many key organisations concerned with preservation and rights such as the Commons, Open Spaces and Footpaths Preservation Society and the Committee for Environmental Conservation, and he was Chairman of the Save the Broad Street Line Campaign in 1963. He was a journalist in Fleet Street before joining the Ministry of Overseas Development in 1965 as public relations adviser to the Minister. From there he transferred to the Ministry of Transport, where he became Chief Information Officer.

Tony Aldous was born in London in 1935 of a family three generations out of Suffolk. He read law at Bristol University, then trained as a journalist on local newspapers in Middlesex, Buckinghamshire, Yorkshire and London. He worked on the *Eastern Daily Press* before joining *The Times* in 1967 to work on the PHS column and was environment reporter 1970–73. He left *The Times* in 1973 and has since worked as a freelance environment and architectural journalist. He has written two books: *Battle for the Environment* (Fontana 1972), and *Goodbye, Britain?* (Sidgwick & Jackson 1975). Married to a fellow Bristol graduate, they have three children and live in a decaying Edwardian 'semi' on the edge of Blackheath, London.

v. A.

Idbury Manor, Oxfordshire

CHAPTER I

'THE COUNTRYMAN'

Crispin Gill

To UNDERSTAND *The Countryman*, one has to read *England's Green and Pleasant Land* which first appeared in book form in 1925, two years before the birth of the magazine. It is a harsh, almost cruel attack not only on the state of farming and life in the English countryside but the people who inhabited it; not just the landlords and the farmers but the priests and the labourers too. Only the schoolteachers get a kind word, and even their school buildings and managers are pilloried mercilessly. The author claims that he is bending over backwards to be fair, that he paints an honest picture, that there can be no improvement until people realise how bad things are. The title of course comes from that poem of William Blake's which the members of Women's Institutes still sing at the start of every meeting:

> Till we have built Jerusalem
> In England's green and pleasant land.

Without the first line, the irony is bitter. For most of us, either not born in those early 1920s or with the rose-tinged memories of childhood, it is an unbelievable picture.

13

We know as a matter of history that farming was in a bad state. We accept that Victorian England came to an end in 1914 with the start of World War I, but we forget that Victorian England, the Industrial Revolution and the growth of an urban factory-based civilisation had destroyed the countryside. The British were to dominate the markets of the world by selling their manufactured goods cheaper than anyone else; they kept costs down by paying low wages which were possible because of cheap food. This process had destroyed the economic base of the British countryside. Merrie England had died under the steam hammers of the factories. The social reformers had long seen the terrors of the urban slums and had roused the national conscience before the turn of the century. But the roses round the door had hidden the evils of the village cottages; the social consciences were in urban breasts, and the worst evils of Victorian England survived in the countryside into the 1920s.

Robertson Scott, who looked past the roses, was a newspaperman who had grown up in the days when to be a journalist was the highest calling, when it was thought that the power of the pen could reform the world and do more than either the politician or the priest. He was born in 1866 in Wigton, a small town in the north-west, and went to school and lived there till he moved with his family to Birmingham and got his first full-time job with the *Birmingham Gazette*. He was always proud of his Scots ancestry and their rural backgrounds; he himself was basically small-town Cumberland rather than country.

Before he left Wigton, Scott had managed to sell articles to London, and he had not been long in Birmingham when the great W. T. Stead telegraphed: 'When can you come to London?' Robertson Scott was 21: here were the gates of Heaven opening. 'Tomorrow', he wired, and in 1887 joined the *Pall Mall Gazette*.

This was one of a group of small evening papers which were more concerned with their editorials than their news. The 'new boy' was set to improve the news content of the paper, but the preaching of the true gospel of radical Liberalism remained the *Pall Mall*'s real purpose. On a typical front page the leading article occupied the first two columns, and a political interview the other two. In later life Robertson Scott argued that Stead rather than Northcliffe invented the new journalism. Stead made the interview into an art-form and was not above the flamboyant in style. In fact, the untrustworthy Frank Harris said that Stead made the *Gazette* 'something close to a yellow journal'. Stead is remembered for buying a girl of twelve from her mother just to demonstrate how easy it was to procure slum children for prostitution. He had noble allies to prove the purity of his intent, but he failed to consult the girl's father and was sent to prison for three months.

Robertson Scott was also to serve under Alfred Spender and H. W. Massingham and earned a reputation as one of the best sub-editors in London. He moved to the *Westminster Gazette* and the *Daily Chronicle*, still radical papers, and when Massingham resigned from the chair of the *Chronicle* because he was opposed to the Boer War, Robertson Scott resigned too. It was 1899; he was 33.

As an old man he was to call himself the first agricultural journalist, though it has also been said that he could not tell a field of barley from a field of wheat, or the song of one bird from another. But in 1899 Robertson Scott moved out to Great Canfield in Essex and until 1914 wrote articles on country topics for magazines like the *Country Gentleman* and *World's Works*. He used 'Home Counties' as a pen name and the interviewing methods of his mentor Stead. In his London days he had got to know the political figures and now he wrote to and met all the pioneering figures in farming. He began too his visits to Holland and Denmark, where agriculture and rural education were being revitalised and brought up to date. He was always concerned with people and their lives, rather than the state of the crops. In this period too he married, at the age of forty, a Scotswoman, Elspet Keith.

The years of World War I he and his wife spent in Japan, producing a magazine called *The New East* with the support of the British Embassy. By the beginning of 1918 he was back in London and joined *The Nation* (long since amalgamated into *The New Statesman and Nation*). But he wanted country life again, within easy reach of London, and in 1922 bought Idbury Manor, a couple of miles from Kingham Station and twenty from Oxford, a high cold house on the edge of a hamlet, away from any main road, isolated on the Oxfordshire slopes of the Cotswolds. The 'tall spare black-bearded man' who had gone to talk to St Loe Strachey and Eric Parker about the articles for the *Country Gentleman* was now 56, and with a wealth of experience behind him. Just as he had run a 'Progressive Club' in Dunmow with poetry readings and plays washed down with coffee, so he tried to revitalise this Oxfordshire hamlet with meetings of 'Village Neighbours' in the schoolroom on Sunday afternoons.

As the years advanced and his beard whitened, Robertson Scott looked, and probably at times behaved, like an Old Testament prophet, preaching the 'Rural Advance' which was his gospel. His parents had been Dissenters and to this background Robertson Scott had added the doubts born of the writings of Darwin and Huxley. The Quakers were his friends but he himself was a rationalist. He had not escaped those bitter battles between High and Low Church that mar the Anglican record of the nineteenth century and shared the old fears of 'Popery'. He found landlords idle, farmers ignorant and labourers broken by their servitude, but above all he found the country priests failing to give the leadership that the countryside needed so desperately. He began a series of four articles for *The Nation* in 1924 that spread to twenty-four, and in 1925 they were published as *England's Green and Pleasant Land*. The next year he followed this up with another book, *The Dying Peasant and the Future of His Sons*. But it was the *Green and Pleasant Land* that caught national attention and Robertson Scott discovered too that his neighbours were not so ignorant of books and the big world as his book suggested. Even after half a century one can identify some of the characters, because the book deals largely with people, and though the book was anonymous the village soon recognised itself. It is hard enough now for newcomers to win the acceptance of the established families; to be pilloried as they had been by this incomer with his strange ways and queer ideas was intolerable. There were stormy scenes; hatred and hostility; the household was even refused water from a spring in a dry spell.

Ten miles away at Filkins, the other side of Burford, lived Stafford Cripps, a successful lawyer and landowner with ideas not very different from Robertson Scott's. He had not then become, as he did in the 1930s, the *enfant terrible* of the Left, or as in the 40s, the Ambassador to Moscow and the 'Iron Chancellor'. But he was one of the early identifiers of the author of this conscience-stirring book. With him, and Arthur Gillet, the Quaker banker of Oxford, and Robert Hobbs, the farmer of Kelmscott, Robertson Scott revived an idea that had started in his Essex days, of a magazine devoted to the improvement of the countryside and the rural advance. The old idea had been sufficiently developed for Northcliffe to have offered to finance it, but Robertson Scott was suspicious of that wayward press lord and the plan was dropped. Now it was coming back to life in new form. It would be quarterly, pocket-size, literary, good-quality printing and sell for half-a-crown. All the professionals, including some of Robertson Scott's old

(*Above*) The old coaching inn in Sheep Street, Burford, Oxfordshire, where *The Countryman* has had its editorial offices (left foreground) since 1947. (*Below*) The 1947 luncheon in the *Punch* office to mark the retirement of the founder and first Editor. Robertson Scott is cutting the cake with the Prime Minister, C. R. Attlee, and the Countess of Albemarle on his right, the chairman of *Punch*, Mr Peter Agnew, and Mrs Robertson Scott, on his left, and Sir Stafford Cripps walking behind him

Changes in farming machinery and manpower in the past fifty years. *(above)* thrashing at Thornton Dale, Yorkshire in the 1920s; *(below)* harvesting at Chilmark, on Salisbury Plain, in the 1970s. The steam threshing has ten men at work, the two combine harvesters just a man apiece

editors, told him that every single point was wrong. What was even more impossible was the idea that everything—editing, advertising, circulation—should be done from Idbury Manor, buried deep in a backward corner of Oxfordshire away from Fleet Street, the advertising agencies and everything else. Robertson Scott had a little money; his friends thought the new magazine might sell a thousand copies and helped raise a total launching capital of £500.

The first issue of *The Countryman* came in Spring 1927. The print order was 9,000 although a lot of copies were given away, bread cast upon the waters, which spread the message and brought future sales. Within seven years the magazine was selling 9,000 copies of each issue. The first issue had 82 editorial pages and 16 advertising pages; within seven years there were 162 pages of editorial and 184 of advertising. Robertson Scott was Editor and his wife Assistant Editor; but Scott was everything else too. He pushed sales with free copies and an assiduous pursuit of reviews in every newspaper or magazine that would give him a few lines. He went up to London for each issue and did a personal tour of the advertising agencies, selling space himself. There is a story that he went down Fleet Street one day with a pony and trap, going into each advertising agency in succession with a punnet of strawberries. The next day he was back on the same circuit, this time in Cumberland tweeds and with order book in hand. The story is almost certainly false, because Robertson Scott was no horseman, but he did send out sprigs of rosemary for remembrance when seeking renewals, and bunches of primroses to prove that *The Countryman* came from the country. There is certainly no doubt that the personal salesmanship, the assurance of the venerable white-bearded figure, brooked little denial.

For a quarter of a century Scott had known all the key figures in agriculture and what he called 'the forward-looking, thinking men and women'. These he enlisted as his contributors and of course he wrote himself. How he wrote! His initials occur a few times in those early issues and a whole heap of pen-names: 'A Student of Agriculture', 'A Country Magistrate', 'Solomon Wiseacre'; but one only has to read the articles to see the Robertson Scott touch. He has stated that he only wrote with difficulty, but the magazine over the years gives the impression that he was a compulsive writer; everything had to go on paper. He had known so many people in his time and if they were not pressed to write for him they were material to be written about; they were all good for a paragraph. He knew the value of names; dukes were among his contributors and a countess wrote on how to light a wood fire. When he reached out later to use photographs in the magazine, he published pictures by Bernard Shaw. A list of the titled and famous who bought *The Countryman* was circulated to advertisers; 'the snob list' it was to be called in later years by the staff, and Robertson Scott relished the nickname.

The first issues were very solemn, battling for the rural advance. Robertson Scott knew that the resurgence of the countryside depended on the revitalisation of farming and plunged with zest into all the political battles over farming. But just as in all his years writing about the countryside he never wrote for the agricultural journals, so he rarely wrote about technical farming; he had authorities like Sir Daniel Hall to do that. Robertson Scott wrote books about sugar beet—the crop that was to be as revolutionary as the turnip had been—and about goats. Goats in the home acre, two acres and a cow—this was his sphere rather than the broad acres. After all, in Essex he had tried to be a smallholder as well as a journalist. But his real concern was the well-being of people living and earning their living in the countryside, the quality of their life in the broadest sense of the word. He also avoided the troubles that followed *England's Green and Pleasant Land*. There are no such bitter attacks in *The Countryman*. Its purpose was to interest people, whether living in town or country, in the problems of the countryside; its concern was people.

The timing was perfect. Farming and the countryside were at the nadir of their fortunes and from this point the path could only be upwards. In the next six or seven years there were to be vital Acts of Parliament and a new confidence in farmers. The cheap motor car was beginning to take people into the countryside in a way never before known. The Council for the Preservation of Rural England had just been founded and the Elmhirsts were starting their giant experiment in rural regeneration at Dartington. All these things are the subject of this book. The vital point is that Robertson Scott, who had been campaigning for the countryside since the turn of the century, launched his magazine and his major lifework at the optimum time. It would be foolish to claim that he and his magazine saved the countryside, but just as when any great invention appears or discovery is made, it turns out that there are many minds turning in the same direction, so Robertson Scott and his *Countryman* played a part, and an important part, in the regeneration of country life.

Success did not come easily. Scott and his wife worked tirelessly. She was a woman of talent and charm, an actress and a writer of ability, and a gifted hostess. There are those who see in her the sustaining force and guidance behind Robertson Scott, and he consulted her in everything. She took paying guests to help through the first hard years, and endured her house being turned into an office. Her housekeeper, Thirza West, a Scots girl barely out of her teens, was pressed into magazine duty. Odd members of Mrs Scott's family helped, and eventually a small staff was built up, some living in, some in cottages in the village or nearby. They were worked hard and paid little. First at the Kemp Hall Press and then at the Alden Press all the girls (and later the young men as well) went down to Oxford at publication time to wrap the subscription copies by hand. They were working for a dictator who could be a martinet and was a stickler for perfection; they were also a young and high-spirited bunch of girls round the grand old man. His wife watched them all like a hawk, but in turn, when young men were recruited to the staff, Robertson Scott watched them equally closely. Any sign of a young man paying attention to one of the girls brought out his fiercest displeasure. The men tended not to last and once or twice there were palace revolutions; Victor Bonham-Carter, for instance, and two other members of the staff went off to Bourton on the Water and founded a rival magazine. But, as Robertson Scott boasted, though there were many imitations, none survived.

Such stresses and strains were inevitable, but the general impression of Idbury is of a house made warm and beautiful, coloured by the strong personalities of the leaders, and its people carried along by the general excitement of a new idea fighting its way to success. As the magazine achieved fame so the great came to see The Countryman himself. John Masefield, George Lansbury, Edith Evans, E. V. Lucas, Sylvia Townsend Warner (who lived at Idbury for a time), Daisy, Countess of Warwick who had been mistress of King Edward VII and then turned to socialism (she had helped Robertson Scott in Essex), the Master of Semphill pushing the merits of the private aircraft; it was a very mixed bag who joined the select tea-parties in the hall of an afternoon with Mrs Robertson Scott presiding.

But the ideas were winning. Within three years of the attack in *England's Green and Pleasant Land* on the tumbledown village homes of Idbury there were council houses being built there. Robertson Scott was first a district and then a county councillor, on the Housing Committee, chairman of the Library Committee, and a magistrate. World War II saw full government support for farming and after the war it was not withdrawn, as after 1918, but strengthened. There were rural water boards before World War II putting piped water and drains into village homes; schools, bus services, library facilities all marched forward. By the time he was eighty, with *The Countryman* an established and respected publication across the English-speaking world, Robertson Scott could feel that the rural advance he had so long preached had arrived.

In fact, by 1943, with the added strain of the war and at the age of 77, he wanted some relief, principally from the advertising and circulation side of the business. The magazine was established with sales at 33,000 and there was as much advertising as wartime paper restrictions allowed. The editorial side was still the crux. After examining a number of solutions Robertson Scott reached agreement with Bradbury Agnew, the owners of *Punch*. They became owners of *The Countryman*, with responsibility for the commercial side, though complete editorial freedom and a veto on advertising was reserved for the Editor and his successors. From the start Robertson Scott had refused certain advertising—cigarettes, alcohol, patent medicines, circuses and money-lending among them. (He had strong views in many directions, and *Who's Who* for this period shows him to have been a member of numerous societies for or against a variety of causes. He supported cremation for instance, and the ideas of his friend Marie Stopes, whose advertisements he printed when the 'respectable' world still tutted over birth-control.) *Punch* and *The Countryman* settled down well together and the only physical difference to the outside world was that printing was now done on the Bradbury Agnew press instead of the Alden Press.

The change in ownership also signalled the break-up of the Idbury household of *Countryman* staff. Some of the young people who had worked on circulation or advertising moved to the *Punch* office in London; the war had taken others.

Robertson Scott's right-hand man by now was John Cripps, son of Sir Stafford. Cripps, a product of the Oxfordshire countryside, Winchester and Balliol, had joined Robertson Scott after leaving university with First Class Honours in Modern Greats. With *The Countryman* he started in the advertising department and worked his way up, learning the whole business, and Robertson Scott was his one mentor in journalism, but by 1947, when he was 81, the master at last decided that he could hand over the editorship.

Peace finally descended on Idbury Manor with the purchase of Greyhounds, a former coaching inn in Sheep Street, Burford. John Cripps began his editorship there with Faith Sharp as Assistant Editor; She had joined the magazine at about the same time as himself as the Editor's secretary. At a farewell luncheon party for Robertson Scott at the famous *Punch* table in Bouverie Street, the Prime Minister, Mr Attlee, made the major speech supported by Field-Marshall Earl Wavell and a host of distinguished people. In the next Honours List, Robertson Scott joined the select company of the Companions of Honour.

The magazine had expanded in outlook as well as size. Its readers were still basically concerned with the well-being of country people and the countryside, but they were interested too in wildlife, every aspect of gardening, the old country crafts that were dying out under the pressures of the rural advance, the rural qualities that were disappearing under the greater mobility of people and ideas. There were also the new threats to the countryside from the sprawling towns, the new power stations, the rising demand for reservoirs and aerodromes. John Cripps's concern had to be not so much to promote the rural advance as to check the urban avalanche.

For thirteen years John Cripps still had Robertson Scott at his elbow, still writing for the magazine, still pouring out words and ideas, right up to his death in 1962 at the age of 96. But Robertson Scott did not interfere with the new Editor; he was content to write. Scott saw the continuation of his magazine assured, its attitudes changing with changing times but its integrity and spirit undiminished. John Cripps was his own man and, like Robertson Scott, had no time for faith without works; he served on the rural district council and the county planning committee, the Rural Industries Bureau and other national bodies concerned with the countryside.

How well John Cripps CBE battled for the countryside is shown by his appointment in 1970 as the second chairman of the Countryside Commission. This was formed in 1968 to take over the work of the National Parks Commission and a general responsibility for the whole countryside of England and Wales. He has since been twice renewed in that office. Nominally it is a part-time job, but being the man he is, John Cripps made it more and more a full day's work. He was also at this time the national chairman of the Rural District Councils' Association. The magazine work became increasingly a matter of midnight oil and long weekends and there was a door at the back of the Sheep Street office always open. Holding the fort during his absences were Faith Sharp, Ann Farwell, Bruce Campbell and Ena Dangerfield, a faithful and experienced team. So after forty-four years with *The Countryman*, twenty-four as Editor, John Cripps resigned the chair to give his full time to the Countryside Commission. He remains a director of the company, and still lives a few miles from the editorial office. Faith Sharp, after a similar period of service, retired at the same time and Ann Farwell soon afterwards, when she became Mrs John Cripps.

There had been other changes. In 1969 Bradbury Agnew was taken over by United Newspapers, basically a chain of provincial papers such as the *Yorkshire Post*, the *Sheffield Telegraph* and the *Lancashire Evening Post*. Robertson Scott would have been happy, for the group had been formed originally by Lloyd George, whose agricultural policy he had helped to shape, and was based on the old *Daily Chronicle* where Scott had worked under the great Massingham. Its chairman, W. D. (later Lord) Barnetson was a journalist with no desire to interfere with a magazine of repute and success. And *The Countryman* was commercially successful—after the war it had settled down to a pattern of 208 pages with 36 given to advertising, and the biggest sale of any country magazine in Britain. In 1955, its circulation reached a peak of 81,000 but the following year brought the first cover charge increase since the start, from 2s 6d to 3s, and in 1961 the price had to go up again to 5s. This, and a policy decision not to push circulation, led to the 1967 low of 51,814. Then it began to climb again naturally. When John Cripps retired that figure was 57,488, and by 1975 was nudging 70,000 in spite of the inflation of that year which brought three cover increases to a final 50p. With the closure in 1969 of the Bradbury Agnew London printing office, *The Countryman* had gone back to the Alden Press at Oxford and offset printing; the 1975 need for economies moved printing back to a United Newspaper subsidiary, George Pulman & Sons Ltd of Bletchley, with computerised typesetting.

I took over as Editor in 1971 with no closer connection before that with the magazine than an irregular reading since leaving school in 1934, and the fact that in about 1938, attracted by one of Robertson Scott's advertisements for an editorial assistant, I had got as far as looking at the outside of Idbury Manor one cold Sunday afternoon. But I was about to get married; one did not easily change jobs in those days. I went back to *The Western Morning News* at Plymouth, which I had joined when I left my grammar school in 1934 and remained there, apart from the war years, until 1971, when at John Cripps's invitation I followed him on *The Countryman*. My training and my life had been in the hurly-burly of morning newspaper work; I had been reporter, sub-editor, and specialist writer and from 1946, under various titles had been in charge of producing a regional paper for a wide rural area, night after night. My home was on Dartmoor where I had done a ten-year stint for the Dartmoor National Park; I had been mixed up with the political in-fighting of the countryside through various amenity societies and so knew most of the people in the business.

It was a brave move for *The Countryman* chairman, Norman Whinfrey, and for a man like John Cripps trained by the old master himself, to bring in someone from outside the fold. But all good publications, daily, weekly, monthly or quarterly, acquire their own character which is not easily changed and which one would not want to change. John Cripps had put a drawing on *The Countryman* cover; I made it a bigger drawing. Over the years, we have both made steady changes, as Robertson Scott did. The years develop and so do people, but Scott's portrait still hangs in the hall in Sheep Street and though I never knew the man personally I am regularly aware of him. It is a sobering thought that after five years in his chair I am just coming to the age when he launched the magazine, fifty years ago.

It is those fifty years that this book is all about. Eleven writers, leading authorities in their own fields (and in most cases regular contributors to the magazine) write about those fifty years. It becomes apparent as one reads that the quality of life that Robertson Scott wanted for the countryside has been made possible, but the things that have made it possible have brought their own problems. Farming has become profitable but increasingly at the expense of the landscape; cottages have got water and electricity but this has meant reservoirs and overhead power lines. These are the problems that the future *Countryman* has to look to. We do not want a rural Britain in a glass case, but we will not tolerate wholesale destruction to save a few pence. People need the 're-creation' that the countryside can bring, but must not destroy the thing they love in the process. We are still concerned with the well-being of the people who live in the countryside, but have to accept now that only a small part of them earn their living directly from the land. We still seek to convey to townspeople the vital importance to Britain of its countryside and its country people.

The Countryman has played its part in the rural advance, and all honour to Robertson Scott that he made it possible. Before we, which means the magazine, its readership and all right-thinking men and women, can play our proper part and take the right views in the future, we must look back over our shoulder and see what has been happening in the past. This the book sets out to do.

CHAPTER 2

FARMING

Tristram Beresford

HALF A CENTURY AGO, the farms of Britain were in a sorry plight. The bottom had fallen out of things in July 1921 when Lloyd George—that 'peasant of genius' as Robertson Scott called him—threw in his lot with the urban voter, and repealed the Corn Production Acts, and with them the Agricultural Wages Board that prescribed minimum rates for farm-workers. Prices fell at once, and by 1927 they were half what they had been at the height of the boom, and still falling. Rents were collapsing too, which meant that landlords' capital was unserviced and investment in land and buildings at a standstill. Neither landowners nor farmers had confidence to borrow—even at 3 per cent. As for farm-workers, their wages had slipped from 42 to 30s, on very short agreements, or none at all.

As farmers lost heart, the countryside lost its bloom. It became a depressed area, marked by lack of enterprise, under-employment of resources and a shortage of young men. Marginal land tumbled down to scrub; 150,000 acres a year went out of agricultural use; and urban encroachment would continue at this rate throughout the inter-war period. In short, demoralisation had set in. Things were to get worse before they got better.

In the 1920s, Britain was still an active, free-trading nation. We believed in *laissez-faire* and in its corollary, *sauve qui peut*. We believed in parity with the dollar—even at the cost of unemployment. We believed that the economic life of the world would go on revolving round the City of London. In other words, we believed in the past, and wanted to get back to it as a corrective to the blighted hopes of the present. Nostalgia persisted until the debacle of 1929 and the death of the gold pound in 1931—the de facto end of the nineteenth century. That turning point had not been reached when Robertson Scott, from a hamlet in Oxfordshire, applied himself to the task of 'whetting the atavistic instincts of town-bound Englishmen'.

Whether or not because of their atavistic instincts, there were town-bound Englishmen in 1927 who were aware of the plight of the land, and worried about it. They knew that post-war policies in Europe had taken a different turn, and that country after country had gone over to tariffs to protect their peasantry. But Britain had no peasants, or very few; and in any case, such measures would be retrogressive for a free-trading nation—the workshop of the world where those engaged in primary production were only 6 per cent of the employed population. Therefore, if anything was to be done to protect the farmer, alternative measures had to be found. With our national predilection for placebos rather than principles, a number of short-term expedients came under discussion. One or two were being tried. Before we come to them, two points should be made.

The first is that although politicians were uneasy about the state of farming, there was no sense of urgency about it. Lloyd George, who by this time had had opportunity to repent at leisure, was now convinced— so he said—that the problems of agriculture should be tackled without reference to party. *The Times* agreed. It was high time that 'an industry, vast, fundamental and complicated' should be taken out of politics. But these were pious sentiments. Stanley Baldwin, who had failed to fulfil an election pledge to restore agriculture 'to a more prosperous condition as an essential balancing element in the economic and social life of the country', was more concerned with defending the Unionist government against National Farmers' Union attack than in bringing in new measures. New measures would have to wait, he said. There was only one party, the Socialists, who had a solution to offer, but it was so radical in parts as to be unrespectable in farmers' eyes. Not for four years would the Labour Party make a start on the new policy; not for six would much of their constructive thinking be made respectable by Walter Elliot, a dynamic Conservative Minister who came forward in 1933 as agriculture's planner-in-chief.

The second point is that the industry's own counsels were divided. Fifty years ago the NFU was dominated by elderly farmers who were sufficiently well-to-do to be out of touch with members in the field. Membership was less than half the number of working farmers at that time. The workers' interest too was weakly represented, unionised membership making up only a tenth of the work-force. Landowners, for their part, carried little weight outside the Tory Party, and the Tory Party, as we have seen, had higher priorities. So for the time being there was little general agreement about what should be done, apart from reducing wages which, though abysmally low, had not fallen as steeply as prices.

'Put a penny on beef', said A. P. McDougall, managing director of Midland Marts. 'Fix the price of wheat at 60s and guarantee the price of cheese', said an Essex farmer with an interest in both. 'Set up a Land Bank', said a country banker. 'Cooperate', said Horace Plunkett. 'Marketing is the key', said Stanley Baldwin, who had a gift for the lapidary phrase, and sometimes used it as a substitute for thought. Some well-wishers made out a case for greater security of tenure for the tenant farmer; others for hens, goats, bees. Some drew attention to Danish thrift and Dutch doggedness, exemplary virtues in adversity. The up-and-coming James Scott-Watson thought the English farmer should model himself on the Scotsman, who was a better businessman and more adaptable to change. Moreover, the Scottish farm servant ploughed four acres while the English worker was ploughing three. 'Is the farm-worker a zealous contributor?' asked Daniel Hall, who believed that he might become one if the land were nationalised. An unpopular economist, Arthur Ashby, believed that the depression was exaggerated, while Lord Ernle, greatest pundit of them all, believed that the tide was turning. Sugar beet, he thought, would prove to be as revolutionary as the turnip—in which respect he was correct in his prediction, though wrong about the tide. Such was the chorus of dissenting voices—which goes to show how short-sighted we can be when we take the long view, and what slaves we are to the conventional wisdom of our time.

Meanwhile there were the placebos. A Land Drainage Commission was given the task of reclaiming a quarter million water-logged acres; there were new sugar beet factories, fourteen in operation, another four promised; there was the Agricultural Credits Act (1928) which set up the Agricultural Mortgage Corporation; there was also a New Cottage Act which provided modest grants for the improvement of rural slums.

The term is not too strong. The condition of the farmworker was a disgrace. On a bare living wage, as an indispensable wheel in another man's money-making machine (Ernle's phrase), he was condemned to low ceilings, small windows, damp walls, box beds and no mod cons; worse still, to inadequate educational opportunities for his children. Perhaps it was for this reason that he was not noticeably zealous at his work. The farmer's money-making machine might be run down, but at least the master could make a loss and live quite well. It was the dreariness of prospect, the certainty that whether the optimists were right or wrong, the politicians sincere or no, there would be nothing in it for them when the tide turned, that drove the workers in a steady stream into the towns.

However, agricultural depression is never blanket depression. There are always pockets of solvency, either because the soil is fertile, or the climate favourable, or the farmer unusually gifted. In England, as in Scotland and elsewhere, there were pioneers: in East Anglia, Edward Strutt, who supplied London with milk from the largest Shorthorn dairy enterprise in the country; in the Midlands, Clyde Higgs, a refugee from Birmingham, who was laying the foundations of an empire at Hatton Rock; in the Cotswolds, Webster Cory, pupil of Hobbs of Kelmscot, an immaculate exponent of alternate husbandry; while in Wiltshire the wizard of Wexcombe, Arthur Hosier, was demonstrating the cost-cutting technique of the movable milking-bail, which allowed a man and a boy to manage a herd of sixty cows. In Devon, the Elm-hirsts had already embarked on their great experiment. In horticulture, the Secretts and the Rochfords were building their businesses on the doorstep of the metropolis; further north, James Turner, farmer's son of Anston Bank, was studying for an agricultural degree at the University of Leeds.

By 1937 the tide was turning. By this time the curious historian, looking for the origins of our post-war agricultural renaissance, can point to a number of events and say: this was the critical point, here growth started; at this moment confidence began to flow again. What are these events? Those most commonly cited are the Marketing Acts of 1931 and 1933, introduced with the object of increasing the incomes of

UK farmers and decreasing Britain's dependence on food from over-seas. 'If you will organise your industry,' said Christopher Addison and Walter Elliot, the ministers chiefly concerned, 'the State will regulate imports.' It was a challenge and although farmers were suspicious and at their lowest ebb, they took it up and voted in producer boards for milk, potatoes, hops, pigs and bacon, the first of which has proved conspicuously successful. Another event was the Ottawa Agreement, a cautious retreat from mercantilism, and the beginning of reliance on home and imperial sources for most of our temperate food. A third event was the Agriculture Act of 1937, a bundle of measures hastily put together to make us less vulnerable to enemy action in case of war. The measures were the outcome of a study by agricultural departments, and the principal objectives were to increase national self-sufficiency in wheat and animal feed, to tackle animal diseases such as bovine tuberculosis, to increase soil fertility, to bring more land into production by draining it, and to get the plough moving again. The Act was a start, if an unspectacular one. However, by 1937 State assistance to agriculture was running at £100 million a year, of which £24 million went in subsidies, and the rest was attributed to the cost of rate relief and tariff protection. Of greater significance were the stirrings of another interest, complementary to the revival of interest in the land, a growing concern about standards of human diet. The work of pioneers like Boyd Orr, Astor and Rowntree stressed the value of health-protective foods—perishables like milk, eggs, fresh fruit and vegetables—for the production of which Britain's land, climate and situation are well suited. Their campaign gave rise to nutritional policies that brought us through the ordeals and privations of a long war better fed as a nation, and healthier in body, than when we entered it.

Here then is a selection of events or developments which mark a change in government thinking about the land. Do they add up to a change of heart? Or are they no more than a series of heterogeneous measures adequate to ward off ruin in unsettled times? Certainly most of the ingredients of post-war farming policy are to be found in embryo in the 1930s. There are signs too, as war draws near, of rapprochement between Whitehall and the farmer. When W. S. Morrison becomes Minister of Agriculture in 1937 his first concern is to ensure that his department is in contact with agricultural practice and opinion. When Reginald Dorman-Smith becomes President of the NFU in the same year, he is sought out by politicians who are anxious to create confidence in their policies. He will be Chamberlain's choice as Minister of Agriculture when war breaks out in 1939. Yes, it is possible to argue that, by the late 1930s, there was a change of heart in national thinking about the land. But it is a fickle heart. We are reacting to danger. We are improvising. We have not yet abandoned hope that normality will return with easier times—and along with it, free trade and *laissez-faire* as the natural order of things. Remedial measures for agriculture belong to the 'Economics of Bedlam'. What justification can there be, asks *The Economist*, for charging the consumer 2s a gallon for milk, and selling the surplus at 5d for umbrella handles? This is the mood. We are still sceptical; and in such circumstances, more food from our own resources is not a *sine qua non*, only a short-run necessity. Thus, though farmers are mobilising in 1937, they have not yet begun to march. When in the late 1930s the BBC staged a peak-hour discussion on the future of farming, it has not yet occurred to them that it might have a future. 'Mainly balderdash!' is the verdict of the farming press, a statement faithfully reflecting their resistance to new ideas. 'Defence, not Defiance' is still the NFU motto, and that describes the state of mind exactly. And yet, by now, there are signs of coming change. Output has begun to rise. The better farmers, that is the enterprising and favoured sixth who are farming 150 acres and over, are making 2 per cent or so on capital invested, from £200 to £800 a year. Farmworkers are on a basic rate of 32s 10d. Most holdings are without mains electricity; most rural dwellings without piped water and drainage. There are 40,000 tractors on the land, but we are importing farm machinery along with two-thirds of our food supply. So, although money is beginning to circulate more freely because of the armaments boom, we are spending it, as one shrewd observer remarked, on inessentials, such as coronation fripperies, not on things that really matter like the regeneration of the land. That will come later, when we accept the hard logic of the situation; when it becomes plain that the world is not our oyster, and never will be again.

Where do revolutions begin? The question has been answered often before—in the minds of men. A nation like ours that has known better times does not willingly abandon its inherited beliefs and prejudices. Old ideas decay slowly. They linger on as illusions, until reality dispels them. But once the truth has dawned on us, then it is natural to start thinking differently; and when thinking changes, other changes happen too. Thus the agricultural revolution, so-called, began not on the farm, not as a response to Dunkirk or Churchillian oratory, not as a contribution to the war effort, but in the mind of the British public. When, in 1947, Walter Elliot made the simple point that the nineteenth century had been an exceptional century, that in the twentieth century many other nations besides Great Britain were in the queue for food, he was saying out loud what the majority of his countrymen already knew. Because the thinking of the nation had changed, the revolution began. Clement Attlee had taken some time to make up his mind and the mind of his cabinet and its advisers. But in 1947 he was prepared to do the opposite of what Lloyd George had done in 1921. Although the Labour Party was the party of the towns, he was prepared to legislate for the continuation of State support for agriculture in peace-time, and to do so in categorical terms. The Agriculture Act passed through both Houses of Parliament without a division. It was the brainchild of the National Government of which Attlee had been Deputy Prime Minister, and now as Prime Minister he put it on the Statute Book. He was guest of honour at the NFU's annual dinner—the first Prime Minister to attend that function; and he sent his Minister of Agriculture, Tom Williams, to explain to the Council of the Farmers' Union what the government's peace-time expansion policy meant: all-out effort, food within undefined limits at any price, production on a virtually cost-plus contract, consumers with ration cards, asking for more. There was never a morning quite so tremendous again.

Even so there were those who doubted. There were those who wanted to know what the parliamentary draughtsman meant by the words: 'such part of the nation's food as in the national interest it is desirable to produce in the UK'. This could mean all or nothing. Others doubted whether the guaranteed prices proposed for wheat, barley, oats, rye, potatoes, sugar beet, fat cattle, fat sheep, fat pigs, milk, eggs (and later wool) were high enough to ensure the objective of the Act, namely: 'proper remuneration and living conditions for farmers and workers in agriculture and an adequate return on capital invested in the industry'. There are always some who doubt, and the doubters within the industry were antiphonal to doubters outside who, like Stanley Evans at the Ministry of Food, believed that the guarantees were excessive and that farmers were feather-bedded. Meanwhile both doubters and believers among the farmers got to work, and it was noticeable that the doubters did as well and sometimes better than the believers. Output soared and with it prosperity flowed into the countryside. Land and buildings, starved of capital in time of peace, of resources in time of war, soaked up grants and subsidies and profits as the parched earth soaks up rain. The cost of repairing the disinvestment of a generation was as high as the course of neglect had been cheap. Machinery too was needed to replace men and muscle. Science supplied know-how, economists supplied criteria. A new race of salesmen travelled from farm to farm. Farmers found that they had to go to school again; they sent their sons and the conflicts that developed between the old-fangled and the new were acrimonious but conducive to progress. It is ever so. Biological rivalries are the precipitant of change. So long as son had been compelled to plod in father's footsteps, agriculture was stuck fast in yesterday. Now it had a tomorrow. The rising generation had plenty to learn and nothing to forget.

The rising generation in 45 Bedford Square, headquarters of the NFU, was a new broom that swept clean. This was no time for sentiment. 'Let him go', said a council member as Cleveland Fife, the ageing General Secretary, left the chamber. It was a dismissal, a brutal epitaph on the past. Ken Knowles, ex-President, took his place; James Turner became the new President. 'He's a genius, man!' was a humble member's verdict on him, 'and Mr Knowles too, I should imagine!' The rank and file had never known their like before, but they knew it was good for business. And so it proved. Ten years, and two expansion programmes later, agricultural net output was 60 per cent above its pre-war level. By then the rural scene had been transformed. The NFU had shed its defensive role, joined the Confederation of British Industries (FBI that was) and moved to fashionable new headquarters in Knightsbridge. 'Our farmer politicians are all statesmen, now', said Lady Albemarle. 'By the labour of the husbandman, the State shall flourish' replied the statesmen—in Latin. Down on the farm, the average farmer was twice as well off as he had been before the war; the farmworker nearly so. The pendulum had swung in their favour. Some thought it had swung too far.

In 1957, the Macmillan era opens. The Conservatives have been in power for six years. They have made a bonfire of controls. Food is no longer rationed. Churchill, Eden, Suez are behind us. A topical cartoon shows two pugilists in a ring. One, the smaller, is labelled 'inflation'. The other is passively submitting to a hammering. The caption reads: 'If only he'd stop, I'd hit him.'

The government's idea is that we should be able to beat inflation if we fight back. This goes for everyone, farmers included. Subsidies are

The railways used to move everything of weight travelling in and out of most parts of the countryside. *(Above)* Cattle pens at a Welsh wayside station are being used to load part of a farm removal special train, once a common feature on the country railway. *(Below)* The early double-decker bus is at Marlborough, Wiltshire; the railways were pioneer bus operators but in 1929 their bus routes were handed over to separate bus companies and Britain lost the chance of a properly integrated rural transport system

(*Above*) Private cars crept into the villages; apart from locally-owned vehicles the 'run-out' to a country pub became a smart urban pastime. Notice the hand-operated petrol pumps (selling Essoline, National Benzole and Shell) in the forecourt of the half-timbered cottage. (*Below*) Rural trains fell away to single coaches and perhaps a dozen passengers but the last day on the Moretonhampstead branch in Devon in 1959, as at so many railway funerals, required four coaches for the 'mourners'

running at £300 million a year. Enough is too much. Perhaps, with a little more of the spirit of Samuel Smiles, a little less of Oliver Twist, farmers could help to reduce them. Derick Heathcoat Amory, the Minister, introduces the Agriculture Act of 1957. It provides long-term assurances until 1962. Almost everything you produce is wanted, he says, but you must take a bit less for it. This is the principle of reducing guarantees. It is not a change of wind, but farmers have been under glass for ten years now, and it is time they hardened off out of doors. The message is spelt out a few months later in a White Paper. What it does not say is more significant than what it does. What it does not say is this:

As an industry, despite your record, which is a proud one, you are becoming over-dependent on State support. Every year, when price review season comes round, you tell the government that your welfare is our job, and that we must prop you up and keep you going. You must forgive us if we do not take you literally. There is a lot of self-respect in farmers, and resilience, and independence of spirit—and apart from that, think what else you have got, what you have been given! You asked to have your Marketing Boards back. With decontrol, you had them, and permission to set up others. You asked for a long-term policy and you have got the next best thing: price assurance to 1962. You asked for credit: you have got the Farm Improvement Scheme. With that, and other grants, you have got the expectation of £95 million of public money for the asking over the next ten years. You asked for a meat marketing organisation—through your own initiative, and with government support, you have got that, too. You asked for protection for the horticulturist—you have it. Finally, you have got an Advisory Service that is 1,500-strong, and free to all. Is not that enough? Is not that all you need to set yourselves on your own two feet, and sell yourselves and your products on the basis of quality (which we encourage) and a fair price? Organise yourselves, so that you can look your overseas competitors in the face and outsell them. But do not ask for more. The country cannot give it to you. It has not got it to give. This is the sense of our White Paper. Will you recriminate? Or will you respect us for respecting you? We believe the time has come to challenge your faith in yourselves. We believe the government has been underestimating you for years.

In 1957, with the bank-rate up to 7 per cent, the smaller of the two pugilists was causing concern. The government was justified in taking a firm line with farmers. It was justified in taking a firm line with every-body. But it did not. *Facilis descensus Averni*. . . .

Ten years later there was yet another Agriculture Act. It was intro-duced by a Labour government that had soul. Fred Peart, the Minister, had made himself unpopular with the stronger brethren in farming by distinguishing between them and the weaker brethren. It was the same theme, The Smileses and the Twists, but in the eyes of the Minister, the Twists were deserving of more assistance, and the Smileses could do with less. His bill was a miscellany of provisions for helping the Twists with grants, business advice, cooperative measures and restructuring schemes. It was well intentioned welfare legislation and it was accompanied by a Price Review that was popular with everyone, because it pumped £40 million into the industry in extra grants and subsidies. This gave output a further boost at a critical moment. In November, Harold Wilson devalued the pound.

It will be seen that by now a not-always-appreciative, a not-always-understanding nation had grown to depend on the produce of its soil, which was, or soon would be, twice as productive as it had been before the war. The nation was getting a high return from a growth industry with a productivity record second to none. It was getting more red meat, more poultry, eggs, fruit and vegetables, more sugar, yes, and more bread than had ever before been produced, and this for an outlay in State support that was, in real terms, only half what it had been when the pump was being primed. What was it like, this industry, with 20 years of growth behind it? Was it the most efficient agriculture in the world?

Not quite, but it was well up in the top league, with the Danes and the Dutch, who had had a two-generation start on us, and whose country-men had backed them when our farmers were unemployed; up in the top league with the New Zealanders, who had a better climate, and the Americans, who had more horse-power per man, and more subsidies. It was in the top class, then.

There was an elite of Smileses, 35,000 or so, who produced by volume half the total output from 40 per cent of the land. These were the big men, specialists and innovators, who were quite capable of taking care of themselves, come what may, Common Market or no. If they had a problem in 1967, it was what they called a tax on efficiency, the pro-gressive taxation imposed by a government that had soul. Hard on the heels of the elite, there were another 50,000 small employers of labour, who produced a quarter of total output. Behind them came a long tail of family farmers—those that Fred Peart cared about, many of whom needed help. This was the streamlined structure that 20 years of evolution had produced—a fluid structure because the number of farmers and farmworkers was shrinking year by year. Some said that by 1977 we should have only 150,000 farmers and 200,000 workers, less than 2 per cent of the employed population, left on the land (indeed, it has almost come to that!). However, on the way to 1977, we have crossed a divide. As one farmer put it: 'We came to the end of the road we know.' We have left behind us the Wasteland of the 1920s, and the blossoming desert of the '30s, and the promised land of the post-war years. From now on it seems that we cannot extrapolate any more. It is only safe to assume that we cannot assume anything. What will become of the oil-fuelled, hierarchical, capital-intensive industry that thirty years of economic growth have created? Will it accelerate, or run down?

Agriculture is not an industry. It is a compact, heterogeneous fraternity of professionals, individualists, private-enterprisers, kulaks; wary, resourceful, practical, shrewd enough to know that times are no longer what they were, and confused as to what the future holds like everybody else with capital at risk. Other things being equal it is beyond question that this heterogeneous group would continue to supply an ever larger amount of food at acceptable prices, and do sufficiently well out of the business not only to replace working capital out of savings but to create new capital for further expansion. But other things are no longer equal. This is the crux of the matter. What do we mean by other things?

We can dispose of a number of them straight away. There is the health of the soil, for example. Are we exhausting its fertility? Here and there, yes. The Fens are blowing away; the Caledonian forest is being degraded by the extraction of two protein crops, mutton and wool; Midland clays have lost their structure and need a long rest under grass. However, by and large, the national farm is in good heart; never more so. Livestock: cattle, sheep, pigs, poultry—how are they? We work them hard, too hard, sometimes. They have their ways of informing us when they are under stress, and we usually heed their warnings. On the whole, they are flourishing. Deadstock—tractors, machinery, hardware—does it stand up to the job as well as it did? Quite as well. There has been a steady refinement in the quality of our stock-in-trade; not only that, but a steady rationalisation in its use. Farmers have taken to mechanisation, and have learnt to deploy machinery to best advantage. It takes doing; but it is being done; and the soaring cost of hardware will ensure that the process goes on. The same applies to all the other inputs, fuels and feeds and fertilisers. Farming is big business, and so long as it is, big business will continue to supply its wants. Technologically, there appear to be few constraints on expansion.

What about human resources: farmworkers, farmers, landowners? There are fewer of them than there used to be, but enough of them around to make the necessary contribution, given the opportunity, given the incentive. It is when we consider opportunity and incentive that we have to admit that other things may not be equal, and that extrapolation from past experience and past performance may be no more than wishful thinking. What has changed then? A lot of things. The decision-making process in agriculture—as in other industries—is subject to an array of forces it has never contended with before. For simplicity, we can divide them into geo-political, political and ideological forces. Of the three, the ideological forces have the greatest effect on the economic climate.

By geo-political forces, we have to reckon such things as the Common Market. Much more important are the new power alignments in the world, the emergence of the Third World—the hungry one—and of the Fourth World—oil producers, phosphate producers, potash producers and so on. They have introduced a brand-new element of uncertainty into our economic thinking. Farmers find that the things they took for granted as being cheap and plentiful are neither; the markets they took for granted have taken on another dimension—a European one, a planetary one. In an over-crowded, over-stressed world, the vagaries of the Humboldt current, the policies of OPEC, drought on the Steppes, famine in India, and other things that Barry Commoner would add to the list, all hit the farmer where he lives. He is no longer snug in his parish. He is exposed to the winds that blow through the world. He takes the *Financial Times* but he is still bewildered. So is everybody else.

By political forces, we must reckon the state of Britain in a period of barely restrained inflation brought about not only by world events but by our own profligacy. It is obvious that we cannot indefinitely go on printing money and overtaxing productive resources in order to maintain a style of living beyond our means. Something will give, before long. Growth will stop. The farmer, who has known thirty years of virtually unbroken expansion, has a vested interest in economic growth. When it stops, he stops. His customers are poorer. He is poorer. He is back where he was in the 1920s, with an enormous load of debt on his shoulders.

By ideological forces, we mean a shift in the *Zeitgeist*. We are no longer capitalists by conviction. Too much welfare has softened us. We have the most liberal, the most progressive, the most egalitarian ideals of any democracy in the world, and of all democracies in the world we are the worst endowed to give effect to them. Ideals are fine, but they are the product of theorists. Practical men do not produce them—they produce results. But it is a feature of our times that, more and more, we wish to be theorists, because it is relatively easy to produce theories, and relatively hard to produce results. The landowner, the farmer, the farmworker, all of whom are practical men, have never been so much at the mercy of theorists as they are today. Baldwin, Addison, Elliot, Attlee, Amory, Peart—all the politicians who have appeared in these pages—whatever they may have done to or for agriculture, at least they understood the nature of the industry; they knew more or less how it worked. But our ideological age is throwing up men who do not. You find them in Westminster, in Whitehall. You find them scattered through the tertiary sector of the economy, that vast, top-heavy superstructure we have erected on the shoulders of primary and secondary industry in order to service wants we can no longer afford. You will even find them on farms—in the communes—where they are certain to be talking, while the goat bleats unmilked at the gate.

The talkers are good at the job. They believe in what they say and because they are so certain, they convince others. If their voices prevail in the councils of the nation, they will excel at writing programmes for agriculture. With the finest of intentions, they will redistribute the farmer's savings, re-house his workers on council estates, tax the landowners out of existence, and set themselves up as landlords in their place. And all this will be done on the strength of no experience whatsoever. While they are doing it, they will be deaf to warning voices, because they believe they know it all, and because there is no place for the reactionary Old Adam in their Utopia. But the farmer *is* the Old Adam. Fifty years of farming history go to prove it. For that single reason, and for no other, he may get the better of his adversaries in the end.

In this cursory survey of fifty years, I have selected six points in time, at ten-year intervals, to show what was happening and what was relevant to the state of farming at each stage. It is, if you like, an album with six snapshots in it. If there were captions, that for 1927 would be:

41

'Farming in the Slump'; for 1937, 'The Twilight of *Laissez-faire*'; for 1947, 'Speed the Plough'; for 1957, 'Second thoughts about the Boom'. For 1967, a single word would do: 'Stocktaking'; and, finally, 'Agriculture and the Crisis of Capitalism'. What deductions should we draw? Clearly there are many, but one, in my view, forces itself upon us. It is this.

The state of farming, at any given time, is a reflection of its spirit; and its spirit at any given time is a reflection of the spirit of the nation. If there is no consensus, if the nation is irresolute, uncertain, advancing backwards into the future—as it was in the 1920s—it will neglect its resources, agriculture among them. Government and risk-takers, and ordinary people, farmers included, will lack confidence to do the things that add strength over time. The agricultural revolution came about because the nation itself had a change of heart. We were no longer a lot of dithering Hamlets. We found our motive for action, our belief in ourselves, in the war. In its aftermath, we had enough national unity to embark on reconstruction, in an outburst of practical idealism. In the course of twenty years, our agriculture (like so much else) was transformed. It shared in and fattened on the growth of the economy. The spirit of the nation was favourable to expansion. In spite of inflation, we found resources for the development of long-term activities—including agriculture.

Now, growth is at a standstill, and again, as in the 1920s, we are questioning our assumptions about everything, including growth. As before, our society is fissured; divisions spread and deepen over every issue. We are sick from lack of purpose. We have lost momentum. The symptoms of failing confidence and *sauve qui peut* have spread to agriculture. Why should they not? If the nation does not believe, the farmer cannot.

CHAPTER 3

TRANSPORT

David St John Thomas

IN 1926 the scene at country railway stations throughout the British Isles had not changed since Victorian days. A steam tank engine at the head of three or four carriages, usually of mixed design and antiquity, pulled up smartly at a platform on which a handful of passengers and often half as many railwaymen again had congregated. The leading porter shouted the station name and wheeled a barrow to the guard's van to load and unload parcels, milk churns, bottled-gas containers, calves, day-old chicks and other livestock, flower and rabbit empties. The stationmaster, who donned his silk hat as the train came into sight, walked leisurely up and down, greeting passengers, opening doors for any local notables making towards first-class compartments, glancing at his watch and eventually giving the right-away signal to the guard. The signalman exchanged the single-line token or staff instrument and maybe a news-paper or magazine with the driver, and went to the gate to collect the tickets of alighting passengers and give directions to strangers. The lad porter ran from the unloading of parcels to close the doors left open by passengers, always conscious of the eye of the stationmaster who would rebuke him should he carelessly endanger the tail of a passenger's coat.

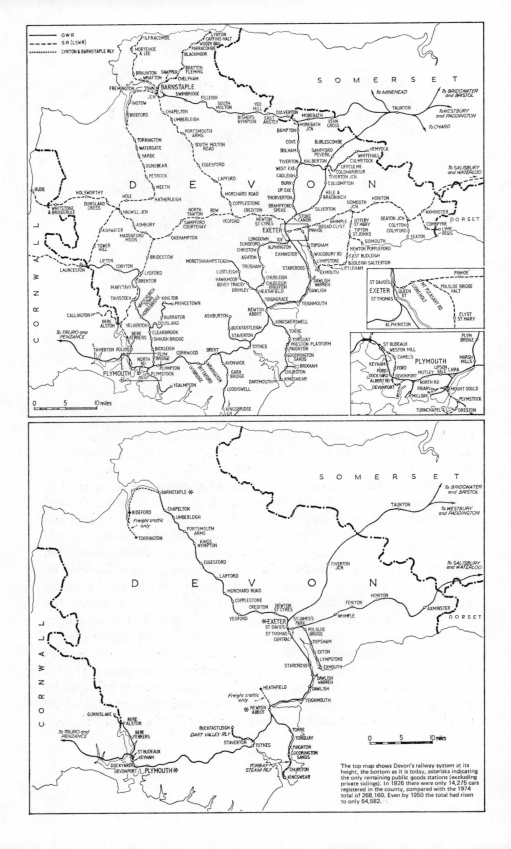

The top map shows Devon's railway system at its
height, the bottom as it is today, asterisks indicating
the only remaining public goods stations (excluding
private sidings). In 1926 there were only 14,275 cars
registered in the county, compared with the 1974
total of 268,160. Even by 1950 the total had risen
to only 54,582.

A permanent-way or signal-maintenance gang loaded or unloaded their gear.

The steam engine whistled, the train restarted in a screen of smoke and steam, the signalman returned to his box and replaced the signals to danger, the porters tidied up the platform and started listing arriving parcels on their waybills, and silence and inactivity reigned till the performance was repeated. This might not be for another two or three hours, though perhaps between passenger trains a slow goods, hauled by an 0-6-0 tender engine, would squeakily creep into the station, pausing with its station truck used for parcels at goods-train rate outside the parcels office, and then disappear into the yard for desultory shunting.

Little had changed since Victorian days and on many branch lines little was to change until well after World War II. Many trains ran virtually to the same schedules for several generations and, especially on the Great Western, might have identical locomotives at the beginning and end of a half-century. Platform oil lamps and seats, the ticket-punching machine in the booking office, the signals and other hardware (now all collectors' pieces) served decade by decade. The permanence created its own nostalgia long before Dr Beeching took control of British Railways in the 1960s and began axing branch lines—and large sections of the public complained bitterly that they could not manage without services that ran at an enormous loss because they were largely empty.

The story is full of paradoxes. Country trains were rarely profitable and, except on special occasions such as the Christmas shopping period or the local agricultural show, they seldom carried large numbers of passengers. But they were the means of communication with the outside world. Only in a few places did people commute to work or school by rail, but an uncle coming to a funeral was certain to arrive by train. New recruits for the Services left from their local station to join up; those who found fiancées in other parts of the country brought them home by train; anyone moving from one part of the country to another was likely to start from his nearest station, and indeed many who had never used the station before did so when emigrating. The mail came and went by train, the local postman handing the bags to the guard. And coal, live-stock of all kinds, animal feeding-stuffs and new machinery as well as everyday household requirements were distributed by railway and railway carrier to even the remotest parts of the British Isles.

To do this the railway had put out its tentacles into every rural area. Very few places of more than 500 inhabitants were beyond reasonable walking distance of a station; nowhere in England and Wales was further away than a good pony and trap could manage in a couple of hours. At its peak the railway system was indeed absurdly dense, wastefully competing lines bringing trains within convenient reach of further towns and villages. Many branch lines and spurs were developed through local enterprise and later sold to the main-line company at a fraction of their capital cost; but the social and economic benefits outweighed the immediate loss. Steam power was supreme, rarely averaging more than about twenty miles an hour on trains stopping at all stations, three to five miles apart. Country services were of course given the oldest rolling stock—many still included four-wheeled coaches lit by oil when *The Countryman* first appeared—but they were regarded as such an essential part of the railway scene that no special costings were taken. The services just had to be provided, at the expense of maintaining prodigious numbers of station and signal staff, permanent-way men and lorry drivers. With their security of employment and overtime supplementing wages already generous by rural standards, railwaymen were almost everywhere the elite among workers, able to develop hobbies such as pigeon-fancying that others could not afford, and valued customers in the village local. The railways paid out more in wages than any other single employer in literally thousands of villages. Little wonder that son, like father, sought the protection of a railway career. The railway was real, a permanent feature in a changing world—or so it seemed.

With hindsight, 1926 was in fact the turning point, the year that ended the great Railway Age: the year of the General Strike, when the halting of trains did not bring the nation to its knees as had been feared. The roads had come into their own. Significantly 1926 was the year after the opening of the last long country railway in England, the grandly named North Devon & North Cornwall Junction Light Railway, linking Torrington with Hatherleigh and Halwill Junction. The completed British Rail system of 1926 totalled 20,405 route miles, or nearly twice the current mileage of around 11,000.

Though nobody—or at least nobody who was taken seriously—foresaw the eventual decline of the railway, the emphasis was now on road transport. And on the roads the colourful pioneering days were over. By 1926 almost all through-routes had been completely tarred—even the hills which had been left rough till last to help horses get a better foothold

—and with the near-universal adoption of that vital little device, the self-starter, middle-class ladies as well as doctors were making calls in small saloon cars, such as the Austin 7 and the bullnose Morris. It was still only the more adventurous who would drive from one part of the country to another by car, and many larger vehicles were still chauffeur-driven, but motoring was no longer novel.

Not only were buses linking every pair of towns and villages offering traffic potential, but the territorial combine companies were taking shape and the need for a licensing system to prevent cut-throat competition was becoming apparent. Long-distance motor coaches were extending their routes yearly and the touring holiday by coach was becoming familiar. Though horses were to plod round with delivery vehicles, and the Sentinel and other steam lorries to chuff heavily along country roads for many years to come, it was usual enough to see petrol lorries drive into a factory, and in most areas a motor hearse transported you to the cemetery.

So by 1926 virtually all the transport trends which govern our lives today had emerged. One must avoid using the word 'revolution' in portraying the roads and railways of the last fifty years. Indeed, I personally have always claimed that there was only one real transport revolution—when man first started travelling faster than the speed of a horse. The railways transformed business and social life in town and country in the generation from 1830, when the Liverpool & Manchester Railway was opened, to 1860, when the system in at least England and Wales was substantially complete. It had of course been the railway that had first united Britain, making possible the distribution of national newspapers and national beers, through its telegraph system the instantaneous spread of news, and the adoption of standard 'Greenwich' time throughout the kingdom. It had applied its 'creative destruction' in a multitude of ways: village industries and mills succumbing to the competition of cheaper produce brought in from elsewhere as just one example. Of course the change was a long time working through to everyone everywhere, and it was buses and cars that eventually brought universal mobility. But the internal-combustion engine, powering a vehicle on pneumatic tyres, has not created new trends but simply finished the job the railways started.

Thus although today many town workers live deep in the countryside and rely on their car for transport, it was the railway that first developed suburban living. Most food now travels from grower to manufacturer and our local shop by road, but it was trains that first made concentrated and specialised production possible. We drive ourselves to the remotest beauty spots, but it was the railway that first opened up Britain for a large proportion of the population. Not a single well-developed holiday resort, with a good balance between hotels and other types of accommodation, lay off the railway map of 1926, or for that matter of 1886.

The transport changes of the last half-century are those of degree. They are important, fascinating, sometimes worrying changes, of course, but they will be more easily understood if we appreciate that we have lived through the finishing stages of a revolution that started well over a century earlier. While it seemed a great leap forward to reach the nearest city, say 35 miles away, in less than an hour with the help of the new dual carriageway, this in reality is but a small improvement on the two hours taken by a combination of horse-drawn vehicle and train since the middle of the last century, when the journey there and back in a day first became a practical proposition. The one magic that road transport has brought to complete our universal mobility is flexibility. It is not just that now the journey can be made more quickly, door to door; it can be started at any time.

Again, by 1926 motoring had lost its first novelty. Even if a fully-fledged garage with telephone and mechanic able to come out and assist you when you could not get started was lacking, most villages had at least a hand-operated petrol pump, perhaps attached to a hotel, iron-monger or blacksmith. Some of these old pumps may still be seen rusting away after decades of neglect.

Traffic was thin, even in town centres where chauffeurs or taxi drivers drove their employers from shop to shop; lorries were infinitely smaller; buses as well as cars moved slowly, backfired and were not for everyone; the tempo was quite different. But the main change in the past fifty years is one of scale.

The figures are staggering. In 1926 there were 1,300,000 cars and motor cycles in Great Britain; today there are around 14,000,000. But even those of us who have lived through the period tend to forget how recently much of the growth has crept upon us. By the outbreak of war in 1939 there were still less than 2,500,000 cars and motor cycles, and only a fraction over 3,000,000 by 1950, half-way through our period. Like holidays with pay, motoring was mainly the prerogative of the middle class. The war slowed car ownership and cut down traffic, sending people who had to travel ('Is your journey really necessary?') back to buses and trains. So when cars and petrol became plentiful in the 1950s, there was a catching-up process as well as an economic boom: 'You never had it so good'. And there was still enough growth left after the boisterous '50s for car ownership again to double in the first seven years of the '60s.

Traffic overloaded the roads in town and country, many villages being cut in two by its ceaseless noisy procession. Garages sprang up everywhere, absorbing what seemed a pointlessly high proportion of the national product. The county councils struggled to spread their budgets over as many road improvements as possible, ever hindered by lack of consistent government policy, having to start such projects as they could at short notice to take advantage of grants given at the end of a financial year or at times of slack economy: gangs of men and machines had to be broken up, only to be expensively reassembled months later; many stretches of road have had to be improved several times in the last twenty years, bends being eased at first, then perhaps a narrow dual carriageway being provided, and finally the section being brought almost to motorway standards with full-width dual carriageways and proper approach roads.

The coming of the motorways caused more concentrated peacetime upheaval than Britain had seen since the building of the railways. Great slices of farmland disappeared under square miles of tarmac and concrete, and narrow country valleys lost their natural contours. The motorways have spread urban pressures deeper into the countryside; yet they have also relieved alien pressures in many towns and villages along the roads they have replaced: once again one can shop and talk in comfort. And they have made motoring safer. The worst period for road accidents was, incidentally, in the 1930s with frequent maimings in the market place and at the village crossroads. Not until traffic was four times heavier were the death figures of the '30s exceeded.

Most people believe the motorways make sense and give us good value for money, but that the system as originally planned and virtually completed by 1975 is adequate. So many of us depend on the car for everyday living that few dare seriously to challenge its place in society— though many car owners share the general belief that rural public transport is an essential which should be provided by right as a kind of social service.

What many of us are far less convinced about is the wisdom of allowing the major part of the nation's heavy goods to make long as well as short hauls by road. It is the noisy, bulky, polluting, often slow-moving private lorry that has caused the most environmental damage. Of course even the milk lorry going its rounds to supply the central creameries (mainly established in the 1930s) delays other traffic; but it is accepted—indigenous. But should manufacturers of all kinds be allowed at once to leave British Rail short of traffic and to clog the highways (including some of the earliest-opened and now inadequate motorway stretches) with the largest vehicles allowed by the current laws?

Once, factory-made cakes, sausages, ice cream, etc, came by train or carrier. Steadily more firms switched to their own C-licence road fleet, often alleging that public services had performed poorly. The same quantity of goods now tends to come in a greater number of vehicles, except to the village grocer who has joined one of the national whole-saling chains and generally does not buy direct. The railways and carriers, including British Road Services, now provide thinner 'sundries' services, in many areas only once-weekly instead of daily; whereas a lone calf or puppy would often have been seen travelling by train, today it has to be collected or delivered by road. The private road vehicle offers its owner the greatest personal freedom, but the choice provided by public services declines, as life generally becomes more standardised and anything tailormade or individual is harder to get and more expensive.

The process of 'rationalising' railway freight began with the with-drawal of the station truck on goods trains. Small goods were now sent by motor vehicle from main-line depots. The number of stations handling livestock traffic was drastically pruned in 1962 and soon all cattle and sheep had to go by road. Many individual country stations closed to goods, though conversely many lines that had lost their pas-senger trains still took goods, until in the 1960s all ordinary freight was concentrated in a few central depots, and even their number has been steadily reduced. Many bulk commodities, often in complete trainloads, still travel by rail, but goods stations no longer reflect the character of the area they serve.

To quote a Devon example, Newton Abbot's goods station has lost half its tracks and the remainder are seldom full, though this was the depot chosen to handle the freight traffic of all South Devon from Dawlish through Torbay to Totnes and the South Hams. Even in 1958 Totnes alone handled far more than the single central depot does today;

while in 1926 the branch-line station at Buckfastleigh, where the traditional woollen industry still thrived, was the area's busiest. Today not only South Devon but the whole county and Cornwall receive their land-hauled coal by road from a single rail-concentration depot in Exeter. It is a far cry to the winter of 1947 when coal and the railway were still king and overtime was worked at almost every station of any size throughout Britain to empty coal wagons and hasten them back to the collieries. There was then a railway wagon for every fifty people in the population.

Passengers can still see much of the best of Britain, its rivers, moors and coast, from trains, though on the ever-faster inter-city routes the trains have no more relevance to the villages through which they pass than the aeroplanes overhead. As already mentioned, the railway route mileage has been nearly halved in the last fifty years, most of it at rural Britain's expense. The numbers of stations fell marginally from 6,698 in 1938 to 6,513 in 1950. By 1974 it was down to 2,357.

Most closures did not come until the late 1950s and the 1960s. Because the total transport market continued to grow, the actual decline in the usage of country trains was at first much smaller than the drop in the proportion of people going by rail. Not until 1957 did the railways reach the peak of their high-season summer traffic, though already the emphasis was on main-line services, and family parties were increasingly reluctant to hang around at junction stations waiting for non-corridor all-station trains to take them to branch-line destinations. Some branches remained busy, the train perhaps offering a more direct or at least quicker route for commuters. Traffic melted away on lines to larger places well served by buses, but survived at smaller places, including those with unstaffed halts only added later, well into this century.

Where the railways fought back, they had to do so with improved services and stations nearer sources of traffic. The introduction of diesel trains progressively from the early 1960s (though again the Great Western had first used diesel cars on some scale back in the 1930s) helped the situation in many areas, though usually only temporarily. Frequent timetable changes after years of stability lost much of the remaining traffic on some lines. A few branches were still active when they closed and have been sorely missed, but throughout the British Isles it was common to find country trains carrying more railway enthusiasts than ordinary passengers. This applied just as much to stopping trains on main lines as to the true branch-line service; the main-line stoppers had of course to be fitted in between expresses, making their timings particularly subject to change and inconvenience.

Many wayside main-line stations in fact closed before the mass execution of branch lines in the 1950s and 1960s. *The Countryman* was only in its fourth year when the dozen wayside stations between Malton and Scarborough shut their doors to passengers. Crowds always turned out to see the last trains, remembering the important journeys of former years and walking round stations, already semi-derelict, which had once been the pride of their towns and villages, their staff entering the best-kept garden competitions and well informed on local news.

Between the railway age and the car age came a brief but momentous bus era. It was the bus that first familiarised later generations of motorists with road travel. The starting up of bus services and garages by demobilised soldiers lavish with their gratuities is part of British folk history. But the legend again obscures the fact that the experimental stage was well over before World War I. As early as 1900, the far-sighted directors of British Electric Traction, one of the combines-to-be, had divided the country into administrative regions. Ten years later buses under a multitude of different ownerships were working all obviously lucrative routes.

The giddy years were the 1920s when the industry grew rapidly, offering quick rewards for the successful, and freedom for those who wanted to be their own boss. The manufacturers had lively representatives and often gave loans to purchasers who, once they were on the road, could run for a modest shilling a mile. All you had to do was buy a bus, publish a fare scale and details of services, and drive off. As one pioneer put it: 'The public got to know the whole outfit'. Some operators combined private hire with regular services. Many services started on a once-a-week basis, one vehicle perhaps having different itineraries on each day of the week until traffic warranted investing in a second bus. The public were enthusiastic.

Villagers liked the buses both for their cheapness and their convenience. Those long walks to the nearest station, perhaps named after the village but still two miles away, could be abandoned. The buses started in the heart of the village at times that suited; they were an extension of village life with ample opportunity for intimate gossip. Some operators were of course village-based; many were long-established carriers going into the bus and garage business, though some larger bus

(*Above*) Women picking potatoes about 1933; (*below*) a Welsh shepherd's cottage in 1951 with its black-leaded stove and wireless in the corner. Indoors and out the old way of life meant much hard work for women as well as men

(*Above*) The old-style craftsmen, like this wheelwright photographed about 1940, faded out of the village scene as the agricultural needs for their skills vanished.
(*Below*) The Council for Small Industries in Rural Areas now helps establish light industries to provide village employment; they carefully designed these works to fit into the village scene at Kilburn, in Yorkshire

companies were founded by sending one or two men into the backwoods to search out what traffic they could.

Except in the deepest countryside, competition was keen for private hire, days by the sea, or straightforward stage services; on the busier routes it was often chaotic, with several operators vying with one another in frequency as well as cheapness. 1926 was perhaps the golden year for the pirates and their customers. Some operators made fortunes; others who deserved better had to sell out to their competitors; many who deserved to fail did just that. Though some of the larger 'territorial' companies had voluntary agreements setting out their boundaries, this did not stop newcomers; the only way of defending a service was to make it so good as to discourage others. Providing services that good inevitably hurt the railways.

The railways were ill-prepared for such competition. Run down after the war, the numerous old companies had been merged into the big four in 1923, of which only the Great Western (incidentally the main railway pioneer in running its own buses) retained its identity. The new concerns were busier solving problems of integration and internal politics, and in developing their first express locomotives, than in protecting local traffic. Alarm permeated them only slowly, despite the warning of the General Strike, and not until 1928 did the railways feel they had to move. Their first step was to legalise their hitherto doubtful powers to run bus services. For a few months it looked as though they would establish a national network of their own by buying up some companies and opening new routes elsewhere. In the event they settled for a controlled monopoly. In 1928 the giants of Tillings and British Electric Traction reached territorial and other accommodation between themselves and the railways came in as equal shareholders in the companies in their groups. A Royal Commission set up in 1929 led with almost indecent haste and virtually no public debate (though the unions stated a preference for nationalisation) to the 1930 Road Traffic Act, which still sets the pattern for public road transport.

Among other things, the Act established a public-service licensing system protecting existing bus operators from unwarranted competition. This meant that each part of Britain came to be served by a single main bus company, and most such companies have steadily bought out the remaining competition as well as taking over the operation of the railways' own buses. Rail-road relationships became controlled by joint committees. In practice both sides refrained from acts that might injure the other, abandoning competitive muscle in the 'public interest'. Thus even after nationalisation in 1947, when the Western Region of British Railways proposed running a cheap excursion to a village carnival, the Western National Omnibus Company objected that it did not like being undercut even on one day, and the proposal was dropped. Though bus services benefitted from the massive injection of railway capital, it is not hard to understand why much of the public hankered after the halcyon days of the pirates. New operators were barred almost everywhere, the area bus companies often taking what seemed a dog-in-the-manger attitude: even if they did not want to run a service nobody else should be allowed to do so.

Thus the bus industry grew up and matured, and maybe even ossified in a short span of years. There was never enough time for natural selection of the types and sizes of operator best suited to different types of route. Only with their backs to the wall, with rising costs and declining traffic in the early 1970s, have some of the area bus companies called on the independents to fill gaps and included the independents' timetables in their own. And to this day the controlled monopoly has militated against practical rail-road co-operation. No longer bus operators themselves, the railways had to rely on bus companies to provide replacement services when branch lines closed. Rarely have such services proved to be true replacements connecting with express trains. Fewer bus connecting times are shown in today's railway timetables than in those of the 1930s, though with many larger centres of population off the railway map the need for the information is greater.

In many instances bus companies welcomed railway closures as a means of boosting the long-distance motor-coach services with which they were associated. In many places the motor coach has had as important an influence as the bus. Regular services on trunk routes and special peak-season services to holiday resorts still carry large numbers at less than railway rates. But the continental coach tours as well as those to all corners of the British Isles which now start from even modestly sized market towns, and charter buses for special occasions like the Women's Institute outing or the Sunday School treat, are really extensions of private rather than public transport.

So short was the heyday of country buses that many market towns did not see the completion of their bus stations until the peak traffic had passed and the rural transport problem began to receive attention. As car ownership rose in the 1950s and 1960s, fewer passengers used even the last bus home on Saturday nights—the peak time when every operator was in danger of leaving customers behind and the reason why minibuses did not catch on. Today many country bus services are subsidised, but services are still curtailed year by year.

What of the rural transport problem? The cost of providing jack-of-all-trade, regular services, perhaps at the same time each hour or two hours, is now prohibitive except on the busiest routes. The need now is usually for more limited services for specific needs. Public transport is wanted to complete long-distance journeys at the end of a holiday overseas, the university term, or the trek to a funeral in another part of the country; to go shopping when the husband has taken the family car to work; to visit relatives in hospital when nobody offers a lift; to meet a boyfriend who lives a few miles away to get to the disco (though the return home will be in his car). These tend to be journeys of importance; without them life is harder, depleted. Money could be saved now, and hardship later, if services were skilfully adapted to meet remaining needs. That demands more energy and imagination than has traditionally been shown by the territorial bus companies, which for administrative simplicity like their timetables to stick to set patterns. It means taking a broad view and using resources carefully: even if there is a theoretic saving it is not usually in the best overall interest to siphon children off from the ailing public transport system and send them by special school buses forbidden to ordinary passengers.

Except perhaps on the longest journeys, whenever possible we go in our own car or beg a lift in someone else's. The country train, market bus, taxi, ferry, are on their way to join the stage coach and the carrier's cart in folklore. They all had a romantic, human side, bringing together people of different kinds to share gossip, delay, humour, frustration, bad weather. Behind the statistic that the number of hackney carriages licensed in Britain outside London has dropped by over half from its 1926 total of 61,000 lies the disappearance of businesses that were once at the heart of local goings-on, run by men of independent character whose ways were recalled for years in the family reminiscences of many of their customers. What small town or village is not the worse for the loss of its taxi?

Even more independent, perhaps, were the men who ran the ferries; the history of many of these crossings stretched back to the days of the monasteries and before. A few have been directly replaced by bridges; most have gone because of rising costs and because people were prepared to drive ever further to avoid a row in an open boat or some kind of delay. It is when you see a family taking its first ferry or train trip for years, having landmarks pointed out by the crew and sharing the humour of local life that you realise something of what we lose by sticking to our metal boxes on wheels.

CHAPTER 4

VILLAGES AND MARKET TOWNS

Gerald Wibberley

DURING THIS PAST HALF CENTURY we have been seeing the rural settlement pattern of Britain reacting to forces which have been changing
both in character and in their power. We have not been seeing the
creation of a new settlement pattern but only the alteration of an old
one. Each rural settlement, whether it be a hamlet, small or large village,
small or large county or market town was, originally, an urban centre
placed within an area of rural land and established there in order to provide services to the inhabitants and economy of its rural hinterland. The
whole pattern supplied the housing needs of the area (with the exception
of the isolated farmhouses and cottages), the daily and weekly shopping
facilities, the crafts and industries using indigenous products of the area
and it supplied services to all inhabitants. In these settlements too were
the persons and institutions that provided the primary collecting points
of what was produced on rural land—the small and large markets with
their periodic supplies of fat and store animals, of farm products like
cheese, butter, eggs and fruits in season (both wild and cultivated,) and
vegetables.

The two main reasons for the relatively close scatter of these rural settlements were the relative small-scale nature of rural activities up until fairly recently and the restricted mobility of people in rural areas. When people walked to and from their work or at best could only use the oxen, donkey, horse, mule or pony to do their work of cultivation and moving things about, human settlements had to be close together. Workers on the land lived right on their land or closely adjoining it in hamlets and villages. Shops providing daily services had to be numerous to serve people who could only walk to them. Markets had to be frequent and local, not only because of perishability of product but also because of the restrictions of time and energy spent in getting to and from them. In general, farmers were limited, as they are today, in the time they could spend each day away from their farms. The daily period was between livestock feeding and tending in the morning to feeding and checking in the evening (say, between 8am and 4pm in the day). With the modern car and livestock truck, this period away from the farm enables markets of 20 to 30 miles from the farm to be used. Where animals and people had to walk or go by wagon or pony and trap, 5 to 10 miles radius for a market town was the maximum area for general and constant use by local people.

One of my most poignant boyhood memories is of travelling to a local market town from the farm by pony and trap drawn by a mare with a young foal. On market day, of course, the foal had to be left at home on the farm. Returning in the late afternoon we had the agony of restraining the young mare from galloping back too fast to her foal as then her milk would be too hot for the foal to drink. No dilemma of this sort affects the driver of the modern car or farm truck.

With the car and the truck enabling a farmer and his farm produce to move much greater distance off his farm in the 'free' period from late morning to late afternoon, it is obvious that the market functions of many country towns are no longer used or even necessary. Similarly, those persons and firms who buy or collect farm produce or who visit farms to provide services for them obviously can now cover much larger distances by car and lorry than they could cover on foot or horseback. If one merely assumes that farmers and all other rural dwellers can now cover twice as great a radius with their cars and lorries than they could when they walked or rode, then one comes to the simple theoretical conclusion that three-quarters of the old pedestrian style rural settlements are no longer necessary to the efficient working of most rural industries and, in particular, agriculture.

During the past half-century this has been the broad effect of increasing mobility on rural settlements and what we have been seeing has been the reaction of each particular settlement—some being favoured and others becoming the victims of greater mobility. What is sometimes forgotten is that although all settlements have had an absolute improvement in their physical accessibility through the development of the internal combustion engine, this has made no change in the relative accessibility of one settlement as against another. For example, on the Welsh Border where I was brought up, one village was situated at a half an hour's distance from the market town by pony and trap. From another village it took one hour to do this trip by the same means of transport. Nowadays in the motor age the journey to the market town takes only ten minutes from the first village and twenty minutes from the second. The improvement in absolute accessibility has been tremendous but there has been no change in relative accessibility—the first village is still twice as accessible as the second one.

Together with this remarkable improvement in mobility and accessibility has come a continuing spread of urban-type physical and social services into rural settlements of all sizes and types and even to most isolated houses and farms. Piped water, grid electricity, radio and television services, modern sewerage systems, the school bus, deliveries of goods and services, quick visits by doctors and a wide distribution of goods across city and countryside have all arrived. The essence of this change has been the spread across both city and countryside of all kinds of standard services. Life can now be very comfortable in the British countryside. It can be argued, in fact, that the advantages of rural living now outweigh the disadvantages, particularly in lowland southern England as many of the services provided in rural areas are not being charged to rural dwellers at their real economic cost. Gone, during this half-century, is the self-sufficiency of the individual rural household and of the village or market town. Practically anything produced anywhere can be bought somewhere else. Baking the family bread, making at home all cakes and pies, jams and pickles, growing all vegetables and fruit, providing at home one's own entertainment—all these have gone, returning only in fits and starts in town and country during the last few years —not from necessity but from the wishes of individual housewives and families.

One thing has not changed in either small or large rural settlements during the past half-century. They are still schizophrenic organisms, as they have always been. As a mixture of different income and social classes it is obvious that they have never been places of concord and harmony even though, surprisingly enough, many people living in city and country think that rural settlements are essentially harmonious places. But the interests of large farmers and landowners have always been different to those of small farmers and tenants and there is a history of tension as well as co-operation between farmers and their farm workers. The established churches of England, Wales and Scotland have usually had a tense relationship with the newer churches of other denominations in rural settlements, with early rivalry about the form of rural primary education. Old-established local families have often been derogatory and hostile to newcomers and a whole range of rivalry exists between rural people according to their differing claims to be called old-established local residents. Once newcomers become established in a rural settlement they quickly become suspicious and, often, hostile towards newer entrants. Fulltime new residents are often hostile to part-time residents, such as those with second homes in the area. There is differentiation between the owners and tenants of private property in the settlement and those in council houses. Though the essence of village living is thought to be the mutual inter-dependence of many income and social groups there is much argument as to the right balance of private and council houses in any rural settlement, and where new council houses should be sited.

It is these kinds of tensions that make a settlement interesting and satisfying to live in. Psychologists tell us that an individual is most demoralised when he or she is completely ignored. It is much healthier to be living in a community where some people are in agreement with you and others disagree. We are all warmed by friends who agree with us and stimulated by identifiable enemies. Many small settlements provide this agreeable mixture of support and threat. All that has happened during the past fifty years has been changes in rural tensions. More new people have come in and older groups have declined in importance. Fortunately, many rural tensions are now more open and better expressed than they were in the 1920s and 1930s because fewer people are heavily dependent on just a few local rural employers, such as large local farmers or the 'big house'.

Over the past century there has been a growing separation of the activities and attitudes of the inhabitants of villages and market towns from those of the inhabitants of rural areas who are integral parts of the rural economy. People in these rural settlements have slowly become less and less dependent on the local rural economy for their jobs, their food or their social life. The sharply declining numbers of farm and forestry workers are found living less and less within the curtilage of the village and more and more in isolated cottages close to the farm or forest, and these are usually held on service tenancies. Most of the old cottages in the villages which were owned by neighbouring farms and other rural industries have become surplus to requirement but have been easy to rent or sell to the in-coming middle-class who want to use them as second homes or who are prepared to restore them and modernise them for all-the-year-round living. This means that there are less and less people within the village who are intimately concerned with day-to-day operations on the surrounding land. It also means that rural employers and their workers tend to be huddled closer together in service tenancies and usually outside the village. They are bound together in their concern with food and timber production and with their knowledge of its problems, and it is easy for them to contrast their situation with that of the newcomers now living in the village whom they accuse of having little real knowledge of how the countryside operates from day to day and season to season. This means that the old antagonism between the outlying farmer and landowner and his worker living within the village has changed to a new 'them and us' situation, with the countryside users and dwellers looking askance at the village inhabitants.

Most inhabitants of modern-day villages would be surprised if they were accused of being isolated from the real rural activities of their neighbourhoods. They would point to the strength of societies such as the Women's Institute, the local gardening group, the strength of attendance at parish meetings and the active concern with footpaths. Certainly these are all enrichments of the social and cultural life of many rural communities but, unless carefully handled, they can exacerbate the growing separation and hostility between the urbanised village and the commercial rural economy surrounding it. This arises because the village has turned much more of late years into a community which uses its surrounding countryside rather than co-operates in its efficient working. This development is related to the fact that the leaders of many of these village groups are people who have moved into the village not very many years previously. Though local landowners are still patrons of local societies they, and local farmers, are less and less active, partly because of the growing disparity of interest between village people and the inhabitants of outlying farms and estates, but also because the improved financial position, particularly of larger farmers, and their much greater mobility enables them to form both professional and friendship links with fellow farmers and landowners in other districts and counties.

The last half-century has seen some significant changes in local rural employment. Though elsewhere we have emphasised the general reduction in employment in the rural economy, there have also been significant changes in its character. Though farmworkers have been greatly reduced in numbers, those that remain have become very mechanised and this has helped to speed up the change of the local wheelwright shop and smithy into the village garage with its petrol pumps and sophisticated repair services for cars, lorries and, often, very specialised farm machinery. All service trades connected with the horse such as blacksmiths, farriers and saddlers have disappeared from most rural communities with the exception of those which have managed to survive or have developed in rural areas close to middle-class residential centres where the horse has come back in the new riding stables. Other craftsmen linked with local rural economies have disappeared almost completely. These include basketmakers, craft woodworkers, saddlers and local leather shops. In some areas where tourist development has been strong some of these crafts have hung on or have been redeveloped and are now associated with the attractive residential village with a considerable tourist inflow and a sprinkling of shops such as antiques, pottery and glass, delicatessen, woollen and linen goods and general tourist 'knick-knacks'.

The countryside has had to cope in the same way as the towns and cities with the flooding into it of gadgets of all kinds made in the cities and abroad. These gadgets, using new materials like plastic, have usually been of a non-repairable kind so that they have helped to smash any service trades which, in the past, concentrated on repairing things for village people. There is no sign that the countryside or town will change its reliance on such large-scale manufactured products for day-to-day living and any increase in handmade and repaired products in a locality is usually linked with a prosperous middle-class residential area or fashionable tourist trade.

This means, therefore, that if local employment is to remain an important facet of village and country town life, new small industries will have to come into the countryside and be made welcome there. These small industries are likely to have little relationship to the products of the

64

surrounding rural economy. In practice, such small industries can only be viable if they can use premises which are cheap to buy or rent, where they can employ local people without having to bring in large numbers of skilled people from distant communities and where the product they make has a relatively high monetary value in relation to its bulk so that transport costs are only a small proportion of the total value of the product. In practice, products in the industries of electronics, plastics, car components and light engineering meet these requirements and there has been an encouraging scattering of such small firms into many country towns and large villages of Britain in the past 30 years. The development of small trading estates on the edge of selected market towns has helped this process.

There has been a steady use of government money to aid this process of rural industrialisation over the past 50 years. Through the actions of the Development Commission which was set up in 1909 by Lloyd George and Winston Churchill to stimulate the rural economy, the Rural Industries Bureau which, since 1970, has been expanded into the Council for Small Industries in Rural Areas, has actively financed and advised many small industries to get established in rural locations. The terms of reference of CoSIRA are to stimulate any development of value to the local rural economy provided that the industry concerned employs less than 20 skilled people and the population is less than 15,000. This Council, which operates in England and Wales but has its equivalent organisation in Scotland, helps small firms which, in its judgement, have demonstrated a capacity to grow and become prosperous in a rural setting. The help given is advisory, technical and financial and, of recent years, help in management accounting and in the provision of loan finance has been very important. The work is very decentralised in nature because the Development Commission, working through Rural Community Councils, is a great believer in the operation of local initiative rather than central direction from London or Edinburgh. At the present time the emphasis of the Development Commission on aiding the provision of new employment in rural areas suffering from a considerable degree of rural migration is being stepped up by government directive.

Yet, even though the government and many independent observers of the rural scene are convinced that new local employment must be provided to replace the older forms of rural employment if villages and country towns are to retain a mixed employment structure, many planning committees and rural residents have been reactionary and mistaken in their attempts to preserve villages and market towns from any change in employment coming from outside. Thus, many new small employers wanting to take a rural location and supported by government agencies such as CoSIRA, have found their efforts thwarted by local objections to sites within large villages and country towns. The reasons for objections are quite obvious on the surface; the new factories, though small, involve increased lorry and car traffic to the site so that noise and dust are increased in the village and sometimes the amenities of the adjoining houses are superficially reduced. Yet, if these objections are allowed to over-rule all such proposals for change in the rural employment situation, some villages will become like pressed flowers—pretty but dead.

What is the best way of telling the nature of a village at a glance? Certainly it is not by looking at the style or condition of the houses in it because some of the most urbanised villages have been renovated and decorated to such an extent that they are almost made up of 'picture book' rural cottages and houses. The clearest and most immediate sign that a village has changed into a community of middle-class residents is the new pattern of shops. The number of general provision shops is greatly reduced and there is a flowering of new shops dealing with things such as antique furniture, jewellery, ladies' hairdressing, teashops and delicatessens, with the inns being turned into licensed restaurants. Buses pass through the village street but are usually fairly empty except at peak times when children go to, or return from, school, or when working people come back from a nearby town. Streets are full of private cars belonging to local inhabitants and to those living in the smaller hamlets and villages around. Often many of these cars are owned and used by people living on the edges of towns and cities who find that they can shop in the nearby large village and secure a range of personal services without any of the parking troubles they would meet if they went to the centre of their own town. The general village store is still struggling on and is used by village inhabitants who have less private mobility, either because of the absence of a car or of the heavy cost of running it, and by other village inhabitants who tend to use it for the little things which they need in a hurry or which they have forgotten to get during their weekly or fortnightly visits by private car to the big supermarkets in nearby towns or cities. So many village shops are now being used only as the shop of last resort by many village inhabitants.

In the market towns, however, shopping streets have changed their frontages with many of the family businesses disappearing and being re-placed by branches of multiple firms. This is particularly true with foodstuffs but is also the case with other commodities such as boots and shoes, men's and women's clothing and even ironmongery. Even though most of these country towns have now got some form of by-pass, the congestion of cars and shops on the busy days of the week is severe and all sorts of parking arrangements are being tried out, often with dev-astating effect on the structure of the small crowded centres. Country towns now sport their high-rise carparking blocks built in grey concrete, though more and more attempts are being made to cater for cars just outside the shopping centre so that the centre itself can, at least in part, be made available for pedestrians only. But this is, of course, only a compromise situation because if shops in the country town are being used more and more for commodities bought in large quantities (and if possible at a discount), their customers will want to be able to park their cars close to the large shops which they patronise. The crowding and partial re-arrangement of shopping and traffic in the centres of old country towns is likely to continue because this country has not adopted the solution, being used in other countries, of out-of-town shopping centres and hypermarkets. These are mixtures of large and small shops covering the total range of what people want to buy from week to week and placed in new buildings on the edge of the town but convenient to the main roads and with ample parking space around the new complex.

Up to this point planning authorities in Britain have rightly been chary of giving permission for a large number of these out-of-town shopping developments because experience in other countries shows that the old down-town shopping centres in the cities and towns be-come blighted as a result of their loss of trade. This means that the partial re-arrangement of the centres of country towns will continue and there will, unfortunately, be many cases where the resulting compromise will be physically and aesthetically unattractive.

Should I dare to use the word 'planning' in a discussion of the flow of events in the countryside over the past half-century? Yes, it is necess-ary, because villages and country towns are what they are today because of people's ideas of what they should or should not be and a com-prehensive statutory planning system over both town and country since 1947 has been used to put into practice the accepted ideas of the majority —or rather the wishes of those in power in rural district and county councils.

And what have these wishes been? In general they have been to allow minor changes to occur in country town and village but to prevent major urban growth in the countryside with the exception of planned new cities and expanded towns. But can we accept a dynamic agriculture and yet insist on frozen rural settlements? This preservationist approach might have worked if there were few people who really wanted to live in villages and market towns so that the only development problem was the provision of houses for those few people who were needed to work in, or to service, rural industries. But this has not been the real nature of the demand.

In practice there have been strong forces making for piecemeal housing development in the countryside over the past 50 years and these forces have been so strong that they have tended to break through the defensive planning arrangements attempted in many areas. The main influences have been the relatively low price of land for housing in the countryside as compared with the edge of towns; the willingness of many landowners and farmers to sell off outlying bits of their farms at prices well above the agricultural value of the land; the fact that, until recently, the high returns gained from selling pieces of open land for residential development were left untaxed and, finally and most important, that there has been a growing wish on the part of many professional and middle-class people to live in villages and country towns, both in order to commute to their jobs in the bigger cities and for purposes of second or holiday homes and for retirement. To all of these can be added a confusion in the minds of many people as to the arguments for and against encouraging residential development and new employment in village and country town.

The picture has been different and rather confused in various parts of the country. In some areas away from the cities and good transport routes, villages and country towns have declined sharply in population and activity because of the sharp reduction in the number of agricultural workers and the movement outwards of people who originally worked in rural crafts and in rural service jobs. In these areas the cry has been for more growth with both housing and jobs brought into the communities for the sake of better social, physical and cultural life, particularly for the existing inhabitants. This has been the argument relating to areas such as the outlying parts of East Anglia, the Lincoln and Yorkshire Wolds, rural Northumberland, the Cumbrian coast, the Herefordshire–Shropshire border and parts of north Devon in England and, of course, it has

68

also applied to many parts of central and west Wales and large parts of Scotland, both north and south of the central industrialised lowland belt.

In contrast, there has been concern in other areas that too many new people and too much new housing development have come into villages and country towns so that they have become swamped by new development and new groups of people whose interests are basically urban. Planning authorities have been asked to defend these communities from such pressure and the request has come from middle-class people, already living in such villages and country towns, who do not want their newly found places in rural Arcadia to be swamped by more people like themselves. This kind of problem and pressure is strong in areas such as the Home Counties, the southern coast, the coastal areas of south Devon and Cornwall and many parts of the English Midlands. In other words, the planning of the village and the market town has needed to be basically different in rural parts where the pressures for development are strong and diverse as contrasted with areas suffering from too few people and too few activities.

There is also a lack of understanding of the effects of these different situations on the social and income mix of rural settlements. Those communities which have had a strong diffusion by middle-class entrants from the cities have usually shown an improvement in the upkeep and restoration of village property but at the expense of considerable speculative new housing development and a heavy concentration of people in roughly the same income and social groups. Although there is confusion as to the real definition of a village, one of its important characteristics ought to be a reasonable mixture of different social and income groups and, if this balance is seriously upset, then there will be obvious effects on housing, shopping patterns, local employment, schools and rural bus services. In contrast, in areas which have suffered a long period of rural depopulation there has been continued out-migration of younger people and of the highly intelligent and better educated. Villages and country towns in such areas are, therefore, left with a deteriorating situation in relation to social and income groups and in opportunities. But the problems are of a different character from those in rural communities which have been swamped by too much middle-class in-migration.

Another difficulty in deciding whether to leave villages alone or to plan them has been the argument that human settlements have an optimal size which they must reach before they can operate satisfactorily. There has been considerable debate as to how big a village ought to be before it can maintain, economically, shops of different kinds, a primary school, football and cricket teams, a satisfactory medical service and a reasonable bus service. In fact, if one looks at the estimates which have been made as to how many people there should be in a village before these kinds of social and physical services can be properly supplied and maintained, it would seem that a settlement has to be 2,000 people and above before it reaches this desirable state. If this is true then it is a grim picture for the many thousands of villages which are well below this size, and in Wales and Scotland many of their so-called towns in the rural areas are below 2,000 people.

In all, because of difficulties with this concept of a settlement of optimal size, rural county councils and their planning committees have dreamed up the concept of 'key' or 'king' villages, that is certain settlements which are big enough, or can be made big enough, to justify most social and physical services and into which most new housing and employment growth will be steered. Most councils in Britain are trying to operate a key settlement policy in the planning of their rural areas, though this has had to be done very loosely because of difficulties with the concept and its realisation and because of great hostility to the idea of such selective development expressed, in particular, by the inhabitants of the smaller communities which have been passed over. Most people realise that there is a hierarchy of settlements in a rural district with smaller hamlets and villages being part of a constellation of larger villages and key market towns, but many are unhappy at the idea of a conscious strengthening of the facilities and advantages of the settlements which are already the most fortunate. There is, however, the reality of the heavy and uneconomic cost of providing and maintaining social and physical services in scattered small communities and, unless the country as a whole through its urban taxpayers is prepared to subsidise at a high and continuing level the provision of modern services to all people no matter where they live, there will always be pressure to provide services in rural areas on some selective basis.

The problems of the village during the next fifty years are already being actively argued throughout rural Britain. What can be done about rural bus services when more and more people are actively sabotaging them by constantly using the motorcar for all their travelling? What chance of survival has the general village shop when more and more people are going into town and supermarket in order to buy all their

(*Above*) Old-fashioned village shops now suffer from the competition of supermarkets reached by car but this shop in Chilham, Kent, also became a public
library for one day a week in 1950. (*Below*) Antique shops proliferate on the tourist
routes; this converted cottage is at Upper Beeding in West Sussex

(*Above*) Whole villages depended on public sources of drinking water; notice the varied containers at the water hole in Crowlas, west Cornwall. (*Below*) The arrival of electricity caused upheavals in village streets; note the double-decker bus and the ice-cream tricycle at North Cray, Kent, in 1937

household supplies at seemingly lower prices? What will happen to the local garage if more and more people chase away to the large petrol filling station for petrol at discount prices and try more and more to do their own repairs and maintenance on their cars? What hope is there for a mixture of local employment if village amenity societies constantly fight all planning appeals against the introduction of new small industries within the village or in existing buildings converted for small industrial use? How can one have an integrated community if most sites for council house development are pushed out to the edge of the village, leaving private occupiers in control of the most attractive parts and of all old property in the original village? What is the future of villages where, for a large part of the year, up to one-third of the properties lie empty and locked because they are owned and used only during weekends in the summer by their second home owners?

Finally, how do we cope with the situation where many professional and middle-class families are using settlements and houses in rural areas, with all the main social and physical services attached to them, and yet are not paying the true economic cost of providing and maintaining such urban type facilities? Should we make all inhabitants of rural areas pay the true cost of their living facilities or should they continue to be subsidised, particularly through the rate equalisation grants, for the fact that they are living in isolated areas? Perhaps the most difficult problem is that many inhabitants of rural Britain do not realise how much they are being subsidised and favoured by their urban brothers and sisters at this time.

CHAPTER 5

SOCIAL AND DOMESTIC LIFE

Ronald Blythe

GENERATIONS of rural apologists, historians, poets, musicians, philosophers and highly articulate countrymen have brought tension and drama to their statements on village society by showing what happens when the 'good life' succumbs to the pressures and demands of the normal, self-centred individual. Hence the mountain of literature and art in defence of this 'good life', never more increased than in our own century, and hence the anxiety caused by any exposure of 'the worm i' the bud'; Nature for the village, human nature for the city. The consternation caused by Thomas Hardy's novels in the late nineteenth century was chiefly due to society at large being forced to accept that such things went on in such places, and among such people—shepherds, country clergymen's children, woodmen, labourers, common soldiers and rustic craftsmen! Society had to accept that villages were as mature in their power struggles, concepts of love, tragic dispositions and vitality as any other form of community—more so sometimes, because everything which occurred in them was usually forced to work against ancient but still potent traditions which the city had long since ignored.

Until very recently, when the isolating barriers tumbled before the

74

inrush of private transport, television, commuter neighbours and daily battering by every fresh urban idea, the countryman who had, by dint of intelligence and courage, developed a personality which refused to accept village limits, was among the most interesting of men. He was legion, of course, and many such people still remain, although villages have been so transformed over the last two decades that soon they will be recognised as containing intriguing villagers in another sense.

However, we still like to think that villages stay put and our present reverence towards them, as expressed by conservationism or dialect-recordings is but the latest extension of our age-old belief in them as the most natural, and thus harmonious, form of community. To describe what has recurred in them recently, that is during the last fifty years, in national terms can only lead to generalisation, and so this glimpse of what happened is going to be concentrated upon one little corner of Suffolk by one pair of eyes. My years running parallel with those of *The Countryman*, it is better that I put down what I have observed and felt since I was old enough to take notice of the society out of which, and for which, Robertson Scott created his unique magazine, than to launch forth on broad summaries of the church or the village-hall on a nation-wide basis.

I will first of all stare back on that time-clouded and yet brilliantly detailed spot, the village where I was born in the 1920s, in a straw-thatched, oak-framed, clay-clumped house of, maybe, the 1620s, though I shall never be sure now because a bungalow complex has obliterated it. All around were grandparents, aunts, uncles and cousins in similar houses. The extended family, as they now call it, extended to the end of unmetalled lanes and footpaths or to various surrounding villages. My village was about three miles from a market town old enough to be mentioned in the *Anglo-Saxon Chronicle* and with which most of its inhabitants were in close touch. A few beautifully cultivated fields and a lot of beautiful uncultivated fields, dense with flowers, separated the two places. They are now almost one place, with linking roads, bridges and estates. Up until the last war, when an aerodrome began the opening-up process, the village lay in its millennial quiet, except for the sharp grey flint church, its buildings reflecting the warm, muted hues of the land. Except for glazing-bars picked out in white on some of the more elegant houses, doors and windows were covered with chocolate-brown paint, and clump walls with limewash tinted with squashed damsons (or pig's blood, some said) to get the much admired 'Suffolk pink'. In winter and in spite of their tarred footings, one could watch the damp-line creeping inexorably from garden to eve. Houses were mended then rather as garments were mended, a patch here, a darning-in of straw there. The prettily shabby effect half-concealed by ivy or ramblers can be seen in water-colours of the period. In fact, the average East Anglian village in the last stages of the 'old life' would have made an ideal subject for the average English water-colourists.

There were two country houses in the village and quite a number in the vicinity, including a ravishing Elizabethan palace complete with fairy-tale turrets, bowling house, topiary and processional gateway. All the houses were well staffed, completely private and, on the whole, rather dull. Inside, works of art and quantities of commonplace Victorian and Edwardian furniture were all mixed up cosily together. The huge rooms were crowded with things and smelled of woodsmoke in winter, and beeswax and sweet peas in summer.

None of them was open to the public and no one from the village, unless he was a servant or tradesman, went anywhere near them. But, as children, we played in their parks without any kind of interruption, and there was one particular country house owned by the King's doctor, which was towered, crenellated and moated, and to which, as a boy, I walked often. I came to love this Arthurian wonder among the sugar beet so much that it became as much a part of my deeply per-sonalised local geography as the faithful ditches, banks and meadows which annually produced certain beloved flowers, peggles, white violets and maidenhair. I never entered this wonderful house and never glimpsed its owner but as I had to walk through its formal gardens to reach my favourite territory, I eventually annexed it, imaginatively speaking. It was only two miles from where we lived.

Many of the servants in country houses, particularly the upper ser-vants, were not local people at all. Villagers who worked at their own 'big house' for many years, or even generations, reflected its standards and manners. Their feelings towards some ancient landowning family were almost semi-mystical in their mixture of intimacy and reverence. Loyalty was as much expected by their employers as honesty and on both sides it was an unspoken part of the deal. Being loyal was then part of the country code, and was a term often heard in those days. In all sorts of homes, servants, masters and mistresses were not essentially contracting an exchange of work for money, but an exchange of faith-fulness, and there was a tacit understanding of this on both sides. For

76

a pittance wage and virtual loss of liberty the servant was taken in to the security of an 'establishment' from the then very precarious economy of her parents' cottage. Although part of the old male gentry code was to be more polite to servants than to each other, their wives and daughters, often uneducated and condemned to a ritualised idleness, could be tyrannical. Servants between the Wars also suffered a great deal from the host of women who 'kept a maid' in the little villas on the outskirts of the market town, in penurious rectories and in kitchens behind small shops. By the mid-1930s most young people from the village would sooner be anything rather than a servant or a farm-labourer. It was not because they despised the work but because both occupations were still engulfed in the kind of Victorian climate which had become increasingly repellent to them since the Armistice. When the returning soldier or the returning female war-worker said, 'I'm not going back to that', it was not the task itself which they were rejecting but its status and all that this entailed.

The Depression, however, allowed an easy restoration of many of the old values and most village people had no choice but to 'go back to all that'. In 1929 the agricultural wage in Suffolk was 30s for a 48 hour week and, for a cook-general, £40 a year. The local newspaper carried advertisements for 'horsemen' and 'stockmen', but the real choice lay under the heading 'Domestics'. One could wander through page-long columns of wanted nursemaids, footmen, parlourmaids, head gardeners, scullery-maids, under-housemaids, companions, butlers even. But whether farmworker or domestic worker, intelligence was rarely mentioned and honesty was taken for granted. What was mentioned time and time again was 'strength'—strong girl, strong man, strong boy, strong couple. The inter-war decades were the last of the muscle-age, the final pages of the unmechanised tale. It was machines, both in the house and in the field, which transformed not only the rural work-patterns but the village man-master (and mistress) relationship.

To return briefly to the country house; to see it either as a local employment centre—or even as architecture simply is to ignore its brilliant social flexibility. Some of our East Anglian country houses have in turn been religious establishments, forts, theatres, concert-halls, political centres, hospitals during the first war and barracks during the second, schools, universities, science-blocks, art galleries and a dozen more things. Indeed, their adaptability seems endless and there is no other type of building in the countryside which can accommodate, as it were, the shifts and changes of the years. What today's visitor to the House Open to the Public would be struck by, had he been permitted to look round our country houses during the 1930s (which was very unlikely), would be the homely confusion of the interior. Adam rooms with Edwardian wallpapers, chintz covers and a Stubbs, maybe, and a huge photograph dangling by 'picture cord' from a brass rail. Few owners were troubled by 'period' considerations when it came to buying new furniture or retaining their grandparents' additions. The average country house was a comfortable old place, bitterly cold in certain areas and in which inherited treasures rubbed shoulders with homely junk. Only in the hands of an aesthetic owner did they approach the artistic perfection which the National Trust now provides for its multitudes of visitors, highly informed as so many of them are by a vast literature. We have come a long way since Lord Curzon complained of a guest who admired his chairs.

We might have guessed that our social ingenuity would have discovered some way to preserve the glory of the mansion, but no one before 1950 could have foreseen the aesthetic and cash values to be placed on the traditional village cottage. Before 1939 it was they and not the Victorian brick terraces and back-to-backs, which were seen as slums in villages and market towns, and they were cleared with fervour. They included hundreds of the finest old dwellings dating from the late Middle Ages to the eighteenth century, their basic soundness coated with squalor. A plank nailed across the door signalled their fate.

During my boyhood, many farmworkers lived in ancient sub-divided farmhouses or in flimsy little Georgian cottages with minute rooms. A few lived in brick and slate double-dwellers. But the novel appearance of six 'council' houses in fields near the school during 1922 were to indicate both the fate and the fortune of the old homes made so long ago out of what could be found in the village: oak, clay and straw. A cluster of the best of these houses lay in a hollow called The Spong. To live in The Spong before 1939 was the bottom in more ways than one. Its very name (which actually means a narrow meadow with a stream) carried with it overtones of lowness, although in Shakespeare's day it must have been the best address in the village, with its rearing gables and flights of steps ascending cleanly from the mud. Now both The Spong—and all 'spongs'—have passed, lock, stock and bread-oven into restorative ownership at a price which only house-agents can call equitable. What could have been had for £100 or less in 1938 is ticketted at £20,000 in 1976, ONO.

As for the domestic interior of these cottages before they were 'rescued', as their new owners say, it was a period-piece in its own right. It had been papered throughout with difficulty and determination in an effort to hide its beams. Its dipping brick floor was covered with a linoleum square and a rag rug made out of a sack into which strips of cloth from old clothes had been pegged. All its other furnishings were a regional version of working-class homes throughout Britain—the big scrubbed table with the snowy cloth for meals, the framed popular prints, the varnished chairs, the black-leaded range set perhaps in a Tudor chimney-piece, the fairings, the iron beds sometimes with coats for blankets—the entire effect, dignified and moving but determined by poverty.

Except for the stove, some of these cottages were as devoid of fittings as a shed, without even a sink—washing-up was done in a zinc bowl. A pleasant if inconvenient activity was the getting and keeping of water, something so time-effacing that it linked us with the villagers in the Bible or pastoral communities in Africa and India. After tea the men would stroll half a mile to the parish pump with galvanised pails on a yoke, chatting and calling to figures in gardens. This special pump-water was 'set' on a cool brick floor and covered with wooden lids or a board fastened with American cloth. On long walks as children it was a tradition to knock on strangers' doors for cups of this delicious water and to accept it like wine. For washing faces and clothes, and particularly hair, there was 'soft' water collected in butts from the thatch. In summer it pulsated with wriggling life and was strained through muslin. There was also pond-water, which people in my present house drank up until 1940.

As one gets older, spasms of self-doubt assail recollective confidence. Was it like this? Did it really happen? Has something so elementally 'earthy' as the relationship between the land and its tillers changed so drastically in fifty years? Were things as bad, as they say—or as good? Re-reading Julian Tennyson's *Suffolk Scene*, published in 1939 when I was in my teens and written by a boy not much older than myself, I came across this:

In 1920 a farm in the next village to mine sold for £2,500; in 1927 it sold for £1,500; in 1934 it sold again for £750; and last year (1937) it fetched precisely £400. As to the farms and their buildings, most of them have hardly been touched since the day they were finished. It is nothing uncommon to find a barn with the thatch stove in . . . a really well kept building is a surprising sight in Suffolk. . . . It is poor in purse, but in spirit it is strong, solid and persevering. . . . It is supremely and unassailably isolated.

All is true except the last. This is the ramshackle market-town-dominated farmscape I grew up in. These figures determined everything else: the way people thought and behaved, the way the inter-war generation developed mentally and physically, and the crisis which affected every aspect of the rural condition as it was increasingly invaded by science, government, Hollywood, the BBC, the motor-car, higher education and the modern world generally. Far from being isolated, East Anglia's social drama during this period grew out of the tensions created by the many different kinds of 'foreigners' who had arrived in its midst with economic ease and were challenging its torpor.

Running parallel with all this were deeply felt, quasi-religious forms of patriotism which permeated life to an extent hardly imaginable now. One strand of this led from the village to the Western Front. By the time World War II had broken out, remembrance activities connected with the first War had reached the stage of a cult and were, popularly, of greater importance than Good Friday. Evocative litter from both wars is a fascinating if little known feature of the countryside but the old army greatcoats, and sometimes puttees, seen in the winter fields during the 1920s, the Brassoed shell-cases on the mantelpiece, the blue-enamel hip-flasks used as hot water bottles and the shrine-statues of the new war-memorial at this time exercised a profound power over us all. On Armistice Day, Anglicans and Nonconformists, jingling with medals and bearing a great yellow-tasselled flag, kept in step in brief ecumenicalism as they paraded to the parish church. My father, who had fought at Gallipoli in the Suffolk Regiment, avoided all this. As a little boy I can recall playing with his medals, buttons and my mother's VAD insignia on the edge of the harvest-field as the horses plunged round and round.

The other strand, of course, was the Empire. Here the emotional emphasis was entirely different. The Empire was thrilling, an all-British escape route and as everlasting as the hills. The very dole queues in the market town would admit that they took some glory from its

ambience. Its retired administrators lived all around us and my christen-
ing robes were especially sacred because they had been made by Cinga-
lese girls being taught 'our way of life' in Candy by a friend of my
mother's. The country schools were hung with portraits of George V
and Queen Mary in Durbar robes, and benignly exotic scenes of tea,
cotton and rubber picking painted in the rich manner of Frank Brang-
wyn. There were also the huge waxed wall-atlasses upon which 'Our
Possessions' gleamed blood-red.

> What is the meaning of Empire-day?
> Why do the cannons roar?
> Why does the cry, 'God save the King!'
> Echo from shore to shore?

the class would sing before solemnly filing out to the playground to
salute the flag. The village was full of flags. They made tablecloths for
almost every kind of public meeting, whipped from private as well as
public masts several times a year and brought out in their hundreds for
horse-shows, flower-shows and fetes. Most people liked to be able to
'show the Union Jack'.

Owning the Empire was useful in other ways. World War I and its
confused aftermath had resulted in a great number of orphans and
natural children. Some were in the still-Dickensian workhouses and
others in homes. All through the 1920s and '30s our village had, perhaps,
as many as a score of Dr Barnardo's boys. They arrived white and fright-
ened, with shining new boots and cropped heads, and left a few years
later with Suffolk accents and excitement—for they might be *en route*
for New Zealand and Australia. In 1929 our local paper reported a
resolution by the union workhouse board that 'the emigration of
orphans and children maintained in institutions under the Poor Law
should, at an early age, be sent abroad so that they could be educated
and brought up in the atmosphere and influence of the Dominions and
trained to take their part in the development of the Empire'.

All the village children did an extraordinary amount of work from
the earliest age. Their schooling was elementary to the point of sketchi-
ness, and the frequently reiterated virtue of what might be called 'the
three Rs syndrome' is, for the most part, a myth. There were, of course,
dazzling exceptions. Whether this true enlightenment derived from a
church, a school, the Big House, local medicine or employment, it was

always also due to some truly remarkable individual. Without such 'awakeners' the village trundled along, unquestioning, and comforted by custom. Education was recitation. The little flint and brick building, squeezed to the doors with pupils from three to fourteen, hummed with chants and incantations from nine till four: the six-times table, the rivers of England, the Collects, Alfred Noyes' *The Highwayman*, the Ten Commandments, the ABC, the Catechism, or whatever, it was 'altogether now' and then the massed sing-song of 'knowing it by heart', a touching notion. Laurie Lee's *Cider With Rosie*, dismisses the whole business with affectionate mockery:

> The village school at that time provided all the instruction we were likely to ask for. It was a small stone barn divided by a wooden partition into two rooms – the Infants and the Big Ones. There was one dame teacher, and perhaps a young girl assistant. Every child in the valley came crowding there, remained till he was fourteen years old, then was presented to the working field or factory with nothing in his head more burdensome than a few mnemonics, a jumbled list of wars and a dreamy image of the world's geography. It seemed enough to get by with, in any case; and was one up on our poor old grandparents. . . . Twice-two-are-four. One-God-is-Love. One-Lord-is-King. One-King-is-George. One-George-is-Fifth . . . we asked no questions.

Many years later, a third generation on, the Arts Council's excellent 'Writers in Schools' scheme has taken me back to the village school—to old ones brightly bedizened with plastic paints and to new ones swiftly doomed to a faint and permanent shabbiness, on account of their having started off too vividly in the first place. The class-room atmosphere is transformed. The children are pretty and floppy. Maximum discipline has given way to casual expressionism. The indigenous village culture is overlaid with massive images from television and from advertising. But when the imagination does get working it really goes places, with none of the traditional taboos to check it. Ten-year-olds listen politely to my reminiscences of childhood harvests as if I had gleaned with Ruth and Boaz. They are genuinely astonished—and I am genuinely astonished too.

Teachers of my generation nod in agreement; it is all coming back to them, the walk to the shop to buy a new Swan lampglass, the cow-mumbling for the rabbits, the scalp being scraped with a steel comb and liquid paraffin for nits, the immense glory which filled one when something special occurred, the fair, the trip to the sea, strawberries, white violets, an aeroplane on the ground, the regiment camped in the park. After I have talked, I read the children's poems and stories aloud; then, daringly, a poem like Lear's *The Jumblies*, with a haunting refrain. By the third verse they are caught and the pleasant old sing-song, mindless and yet gripping, fills the room. 'More!' they shout, where once their heads would have been splitting from the incantatory treadmill known as school. I—and a number of other writers newly experiencing them in their present guise, via the Arts Council's scheme, am intrigued by the good village school, and by some of the rural comprehensives, though less because of current educational methods than their ability to present such an interesting individual as (in all his and her variety) the ordinary country child.

The church in the village and the village church are not quite the same thing. Generations of insistence that they are, or the assumption that they are, have caused confusion enough in their day. Each centres and proclaims a spirituality. The building itself is miraculously accommodating and can incorporate every architectural idea from Saxon long-and-short work to Space Age aluminium without fuss. Similarly, every shift of theology from Anselm to Coggan eventually finds expression in it without being able to add or detract from some final truthfulness in its fabric. It is also the most controversial structure in the village, a flagrant witness to all its pride and injustice, as well as to its goodness. Nearly a thousand years of births, deaths and marriages, litigation, prayer, philosophy, music, vanity, sanctity and toil are pivoted upon our village church, as they are on most. Countrymen like my father venerated it and doubted whether God was as potent anywhere else. He and mother had bowled up to it in the vicarage brougham, its handles tied with ribbons, to be wed in 1920. When we lived three miles away, he would suddenly take it into his head to worship there and we would set off, walking most of the way across unfarmed farms, to Evensong.

All around were the spectacular wool-churches with their little congregations dotted about in vast naves. People sat—and often still do—where their fathers had sat, thus unconsciously preserving the ground-plan of natural subordination as it applied to rural society a century ago. In Little Easton Church, Essex, when I was twenty, I saw an actual 'rank plan' drawn on a card in the vestry, the peer and his family in front, and ranged behind him with Proustian nicety the village in its exact social order, which included upper and lower servants, and subtle distinctions concerning gentry and yeomen. Labourers came last.

Most Suffolk villages have a double culture stemming from Anglicanism and Dissent, and this is still quite distinctive. Religion arouses the kind of cantankerousness in its village practitioners as is summed-up in our local motto 'Do different'—this or a reserved silence. At its simple best, and it often reaches this standard, a service in a country church has always been a profoundly beautiful experience. One can see why this should be so when one reads the language of Cranmer, King James's translators and the hymn-writers, but not when one attempts to analyse what those speaking them actually believe. The whole of the English Church is now in the midst of a kind of creative crisis, with the clergy victimised by their old middle-class image; and their once discreetly paid stipends, because of inflation, requiring supplementation by their parish, or parishes, for some have as many as eight and few less than three.

Against the lovely formal worship patterns of the English post-Reformation and the man-power crisis surge all the stimulating ideas and actions released across modern Christendom by Vatican II. The best thing it has done is to destroy or invalidate much of the old parochial introversion. Deanery synods, the union of church councils, the need to be imaginative and inventive in an area which was, until recently, steeped in reaction and convention—all this is beginning to affect the thinking of the countryside at large. One or two of our parish churches have been made redundant, a not so astounding thing as many like to think, as the whole county is full of abandoned religious buildings. But to close the door of an old village church, as I did, as its last churchwarden since churchwardens were invented, this year, is a very thought-provoking action. Even if one accepts what Marcus Aurelius said —'Everything is only for a day, both that which remembers and that which is remembered.'

Rural change in the social sense has been as multifarious as a sunburst this half-century, with burnt-out customs, and methods and thinking falling away, and dynamic forces sparking-in to take their place. Some of the dynamism has been rough and destructive, and we are now beginning to regret what it has taken from us, but much of it has civilised us. To catalogue even such changes as a single pair of eyes have witnessed would need a book and not a chapter, and the wonder, when one begins to list them, is that anything approaching the appearance of the old structure of village life remains. Yet it does and, what is even stranger, it is plain to see. One good reason for our seeing it so distinctly is that we are now so well informed on what to look for. That wistful cliché about whether we were happier 'then than now' really asks a pointless question.

Before a Mrs Hoodless of Ontario urged countrywomen to meet each other, thus eventually creating the Women's Institutes, before tractors and fertilisers, before 'the 'lectric', before tap-water and tap-entertainment, private transport, the weekly library-van, the much maligned health service (let anyone over forty look back at rural medicine as it existed in the 1930s!), real wages, etc, happiness existed within another context. No longer possessing this context, our present village happiness is not comparable. Neither is our stress, nor are many of our questions. Whatever happens in the next fifty years, we are unlikely as a society to see such tremendous changes again, only permutations of what we now have, and what we have already taken for granted. We ourselves will grow into this reformed villageship because of the intimacies decreed by a situation where two or three hundred human beings can exist with most of the luxuries of the town amidst fields which do not require most of their life's strength to work. In puritan East Anglia we shall always feel a bit guilty about this.

CHAPTER 6

LOCAL GOVERNMENT

Charles Arnold-Baker

BETWEEN 1926 and 1976 there was an administrative revolution. It was carried through by fits and starts and interrupted by the great slump of 1929 to 1931, by war and by the swaying fortunes of political controversy, but it was a revolution nevertheless. In 1975 it was probably still not spent, for the old order was appropriate to the mighty centre of a world empire and nourished from afar, whereas the modern dispensation belongs to a lesser power reduced in prestige and resources and struggling with diminished confidence and increased introspection to maintain a standard of living appropriate to older glories.

The systems of 1926 fitted the assumption that the welfare of the people should, by and large be sustained by their own efforts and the profits of foreign investment, and that public authority should intervene as little as possible. The administrative arrangements reflected this outlook. Britain was the least bureaucratic state in Europe. Money, it was supposed, should 'fructify in the pockets of the people'. Taxes and rates, by modern standards, were very low. This, in the rural areas, was fortunate, for agriculture was depressed by mass imports of cheap north American grain, under a free trade policy designed to feed the urban industrial masses. The prosperous-looking manor houses of the surviving gentry were maintained on industrial investments. Agriculture, the financial backbone of the Victorian rural administration, still paid reduced rates, but by 1929 it was derated altogether. Thus local finance depended throughout the land on the rating of buildings, concentrated, in the nature of things in towns where administration might be carried on easily, and scattered thinly in the country where it was more difficult.

Elected rural local government in England and Wales was never designed for such a financial regime. Inside the counties there were county boroughs not subject to the rule of the county council, and their rateable resources were not accessible for county finance. There were 658 rural districts, but embedded in these were nearly 1,000 municipal boroughs and urban districts under their own authorities and, similarly, their resources were not accessible to the rural district councils. The rural districts were divided into about 11,000 parishes of which 7,100 had councils, but the resources (that is the rateable buildings) in many of them were so sparse that nearly 2,000 of these councils every year reported no financial transactions at all.

Though the details differed, especially in the absence of a Scottish rural district authority or a Northern Irish parish, the Scottish and Northern Irish systems were based upon similar principles and geography with comparable results, exaggerated in rural Scotland by the emptiness of much of the landscape.

By any standards most of the urban areas (whether urban district, boroughs or Scottish burghs) were part of the rural scene, owing their livelihood and activity to their practical unity with the adjacent countryside. Many were villages where farmers and farm labourers lived; out of 784 English and Welsh urban districts 706 had fewer than 20,000 inhabitants. The smallest, Kirklington-cum-Upsland, had 246. The total population of these countryfied urban authorities was about 850,000 and that of the rural districts about 7,500,000. Under a uniform system the urban areas should, in theory, have brought relief to the scattered rurals in the shape of uncommitted resources, and one might have expected rural pressure towards an amalgamation of the two dispensations. There was, in fact, no such pressure: the impetus towards unification came from the opposite direction, and it is instructive to see why.

The nation had suffered intermittently but at times spectacularly from cholera, and other epidemics throughout the centuries. After the

Napoleonic wars it was slowly realised that these disasters could never be forestalled as long as great (and rapidly growing) concentrations of population had to live with polluted water and without proper sanitation. Boroughs and Scottish burghs, reformed in the 1830s, were already beginning, perforce, to sewer and pave, but these corporations were in places dictated by the accidents of medieval politics, and had mostly been created for reasons quite unconnected with local administration. There were unorganised concourses of people in other places too. Urban sanitary districts began to be set up; these achieved a constitutional uniformity in 1875, and were converted into urban districts in 1894. In Scotland the equivalent of the urban district was the police burgh: the word 'police' being, in this case, used in the sense of 'improvement'.

Thus the essentially Victorian local government system originated as a form of preventive medicine. 'Boroughs' it has been said, 'had property in the middle ages. Urban districts had drains in the nineteenth century.' The opposition on the Public Health bill in 1874 stigmatised the government's policy as a 'policy of sewage'. They were perfectly right, and the emphasis was so strong that textbook writers were at a loss for titles; as late as 1945 one major legal work on local government still classified libraries under public health.

Thus a feature in 1926 of the dichotomy was that since sewers and water pipes had cost a lot of money, the urban rateable resources were encumbered with substructure debt: and in the rural areas these installations, by reason of distances and derating, were beyond the pockets of the rural authorities. In a low wage economy the result was a kind of stagnation: not much had been expected of the district level authorities and they mostly did as little as they could. Most district and borough councils employed their chief officer (the Clerk) on a part-time basis. He was usually a local solicitor.

Into this peaceful seeming world the need for housing had introduced an unquiet element, for houses were, by and large required in the urban areas. Ever since 1890 the urban authorities had grappled with overcrowding and slums. There had, as always in war, been a cessation of building between 1914 and 1919 when under the slogan 'Homes fit for Heroes' the authorities were legally obliged to build; the government undertook to recoup their losses, and the loan debt of local government rapidly expanded. The programme got going (with hiccoughs) in the towns, but 'losses' which the government underwrote did not include substructure costs. The debts of the urban authorities grew; their rate

(*Above*) Country roads were already becoming crowded by motorists and motor cycles with sidecars in the years before 1939. (*Below*) The seaside was the main goal and the picture below of Camber Sands, East Sussex, in 1934 shows that the beach itself provided the car park if the sand were firm enough. The bathing belle left shows the fashionable rig

(*Above*) Hiking became a craze in the 1930s and has kept its popularity; these youngsters are climbing up from South Darenth, Kent, on Easter Monday 1956. (*Below*) Car rallies and motor cycle scrambles also became a sport in their own right attracting large crowds

poundages rose, and their ratepayers began to look with uninformed longing at the lower rates paid just across the boundary. In 1923 the method of central finance had to be altered to a flat payment of £6 a house per year for 20 years; in 1924 it had to go up to £9 for 40 years. In 1923, however, the rural scene had been visibly altered, because agriculture was derated from 50 per cent to 75 per cent. To avoid wrecking the housing policy the Act of 1924 invented the 'agricultural parish', a parish with under 50 persons per 100 acres where agricultural land amounted to at least 25 per cent of the annual value. Here subsidies might be paid at £12 10s instead of £9 on new houses.

Thus in the resumed agricultural slump the policy of subsidising the rural areas by manipulating local government finance had in 1925 already begun. In 1926 it was carried a stage further: the government undertook to bear half the cost of reconstructing and improving old cottages. This really meant that the struggle to provide rural piped water, gas, and electricity had temporarily been given up. In Great Britain in 1926 public utilities served only the fringes of the rural areas: only about 40 per cent of the whole country was electrified: nearly all the 300 water, 200 electricity and 180 gas undertakings belonged to urban authorities. Longcross, a village in Surrey only 20 miles from London, was composed wholly of Victorian gentlemen's houses and attached tied cottages. None had gas or electricity; most pumped their water up from a well. The lady in the village shop ran the telephone exchange, and could tell callers if a call was worthwhile.

In one, not to be overstated, sense the distinction between the English urban and rural areas was a social one. The boroughs had had a fairly new habit of electoral representation, in which tradespeople could raise their status and enlarge their personality by dabbling in local politics; some of this had rubbed off onto the urban districts. Until 1894, however, rural administration had been supervised and mostly run by the justices of the peace, who were nominated by that remote and fatherly figure, the Lord Lieutenant. They also administered petty justice and, in a country where courts of law were still respected, they had prestige. They stood for election in the new county and rural district councils where they and their like continued to serve as councillors as well as justices. Many were greater or lesser landowners who had to get on well with their tenants to make the land pay at all. Moreover the rural district councils, but not the towns, administered the Poor Law. They were often on closer social terms with their tenants (by way of cricket, racing and the hounds) than the town councillors were with their business employees. They had had sound practical reasons for looking after the health and employment of their servants and their families, who would otherwise be cast on the poor rates, so much of which the property owners themselves paid. There was an ethic, partly based on self interest, amongst such people about the treatment of servants and tenants, even if the odd-man-out got shorter shrift than he sometimes deserved. Mostly (but not always) Tory in their national party allegiance, the older gentry were practical or pragmatic rather than conservative in their local policies, which sometimes had radical effects. Under their calm influence not all was stationary. Roads were being metalled and bridges, as at Hampton Court, rebuilt. Of the many local acts passed in 1926, 16 were promoted for various purposes in predominantly country districts: 8 for whole counties, and 8 for rural areas.

The first major organisational change came with the Local Government Acts 1929 and their *sequelae*. The Poor Law administration was taken away from the English rural districts, and agricultural land was wholly derated. Twenty-nine bigger urban districts had successfully petitioned for borough charters by 1936. In the country, however, amalgamations reduced the number of rural districts from 658 to 492, but they also annexed 88 urbans. Some of these were awkward bedfellows. The rural district councillors for the former urban district of Battle were still out of step in the 1960s; and not all the very small urban authorities disappeared: Llanwyrtid Wells with 450 and Montgomery with 980 were only the smallest of 48 villages of urban status which survived with less than 3,000 inhabitants until 1974.

In Scotland the 1929 reform took a different course. Between the parishes and the counties there had never been a district organism. The small burghs lived on as islands in a rural sea, and many were very small indeed: as late as 1975, 72 had less than 3,000 people. New Galloway had 334 inhabitants. But in 1928 it was resolved to abolish the parish councils and, having disposed of the Poor Law, to commit the surviving rural business to the county councils, whose areas were in some cases (such as Ross and Cromarty) vast. There were protests, and the government had a second thought. At the last moment districts were set up with councils partly elected and partly appointed by the county councils. To these the weak powers of the parish councils (which were weaker than their English counterparts) were committed. The result was 201 (later 197) districts which amounted functionally to no more than parishes, but which lacked the saving advantage of small-scale community interest. In theory county functions could be delegated to them. In practice it seldom happened. A Dumfriesshire county convenor was resolute: it would never happen in his time.

It was hoped that these rationalisations, especially in English middle-tier administration, might, in the early 1930s, offset the consequences of derating (which also affected industry) and the contemporary economic slump. These hopes were vain.

World War I had brought much motor traffic to the roads: since 1909 the revenue from the rising numbers of motor vehicles and driving licences had been paid into a government Road Fund which would thus automatically expand. Drivers and vehicles indeed increased, but the damage which they did increased far more rapidly; the cost of repairing even local roads was by 1926 (when the government started raiding the Road Fund) beyond the resources of the districts. The old argument against parochial highway maintenance now recurred in another form. Why should a rural district pay for damage mostly done by vehicles from somewhere else? In 1929, the roads were transferred to the counties.

So far so good, but the speed and weight of the new traffic necessitated a new kind of road with more solid foundations, better surfaces, longer vistas, more traffic lanes. The wood block carriageways of town streets and the dusty macadam of the rolling country road collapsed under the attack, not only of the motor car but of the increasingly noisy motorists' lobby. The deer must no longer leap carelessly over Devon hedges. Roads added to accumulated loan debts, which rose from £917m to £1570m between 1924 and 1934. By 1936 the county councils were feeling the strain too; the Road Fund ceased to function as a fund, and the government took over responsibility for a network of national routes known as trunk roads.

The social and economic effects of the new roads policy were wide and deep. On any cost benefit analysis the motor car was being subsidised, and started to eat into the revenues of the very complete railway system handed down from the horse and buggy era. By 1938 only the Southern Railway Co was paying an ordinary dividend. A central department (other than the Post Office) was now directly engaged in local administration. Local and national highway costs not only rocketed, but road widening, carbon monoxide and noise changed the aspect, ecology and habits of the countryside. Walls, hedges and sometimes housing went down to make way for more concrete. The lords of the wheel were the lords of creation, and most of them came from the towns, now reviving in the post-depression commercial upswing.

They rather liked the country, and those who had made a little money began to lay it out in a little place of their own. This was not new, but the manner of it was. Land on the whole was cheap, and a landowner could get good money by selling plots with a road frontage (hedges already down) and contractors did nicely putting up house upon identical house on the sites. This was the golden, or rather black, age of ribbon development whose semi-detached effects are still conspicuous. In 1927 western London ended at Chiswick: by 1937 it seemed to have spread ten miles along the Great West Road. An attempt to control it in 1936 merely led to ingenious circumventions. Efforts to prevent the countryside near the metropolis from disappearing altogether brought the Green Belt Act. The townsman's blood was up. He was not going to have his vista spoiled by other b . . . s building houses. It was ribbon development which convinced ordinary people of the need for town and country planning.

Meanwhile, however, the suburbs of many larger towns were spreading into the technically rural areas outside, and there was a growing need for rural workers' housing and rehousing. The government provided yet more money for subsidies in 1938, and battles, if such be the right word for so gentlemanly an exercise, were developing at the margins. A borough boundary could be altered only by a local Bill or, for Scotland, a special procedure order in parliament. A real or feigned shortage of land sometimes induced boroughs to lay out housing estates in the surrounding countryside where the land was cheap. On the ground that the borough was losing rateable value by exporting the population, a Bill would be presented to parliament to take in the built-up area. In the preamble to the Glasgow Boundaries Order 1937, for example, it was explained that there is no building land in the burgh, that the territory which the corporation wants includes land suitable for housing development, and that existing developments there have a community of interest with the burgh. It then lets the cat out of the bag: the burgh has purchased land there.

In 1936 Hastings, Eastbourne and Cardiff were extended; in 1937 Nuneaton and Plymouth; in 1938 Luton, Exeter and Bootle. There were similar numbers of extensions in Scotland. After a wartime moratorium, the process accelerated. For example, in 1950 thirteen urban authorities took in parts of rural areas; in 1951 nine; in 1952 seven. The rural authorities generally got the worst of it. The interesting point is that Parliament still thought it right to make time for these territorial minutiae. The integrity and, by implication the independence of local authorities was still a principle over which Parliament thought it proper to watch.

But the fact that it was the end of an era was discernible. In the first place compulsory purchase was becoming easier: a local Act was needed until 1875; then until 1909 an order of the local government board subject to parliamentary confirmation. Thereafter local authorities could sometimes make orders which needed only a minister's confirmation. Such proceedings, repugnant to the spirit of old England, were becoming much commoner too. Widespread road widening accustomed people to their use. Family solicitors shook their heads.

Secondly, another incursion had been made into the domain of rural property by the introduction of a form of town and country planning in 1932. There had been urban planning legislation in 1909, 1919, 1925 and 1929 (which was repealed). Now district councils could prepare and make enforceable planning schemes which required central approval; before these came into effect (which might be a long time hence) the Minister of Health could make interim development orders, under which the councils could give or withhold planning permission in given classes of cases. Permission amounted to a guarantee of compensation if a development turned out to be inconsistent with the eventual scheme.

Thirdly, as has already been noticed, local and central government finance were becoming entangled, and recurrent government grants had begun to replace local revenue. The issue was already connected with borrowing. If the 'Englishman paid his taxes in sorrow, but his rates in anger', the uninterruptedly rising cost of servicing accumulated loan debt made it politically essential to find money for other things from the less infuriating source.

Fourthly increased activity was creating work which needed staff. Somebody had to plan, build and let the growing number of houses and collect the rents; somebody had to plan, construct and mend the new roads; somebody had to prepare and administer the new planning schemes, and make the calculations required by the more complicated finance, and do something about the lengthening list of special powers and obligations imposed by law: who actually kept the statutory map of sewers up to date, or ensured that new buildings really were provided with all necessary drains? Local authorities were becoming substantial employers, and were gaining the confidence which the command of labour forces brings. One consequence was a further ramification of activities: for example in the 1930s there was a great advance in the provision of public libraries; by 1937 the commercial lending libraries were feeling the draught and public librarians were emerging from the dust of the caretaker's cubby hole into the dignity of professional office. The public library system stands wholly to the credit of local government itself, owing nothing to central departments even by way of encouragement or advice.

The first effect of war in 1939, of course, was that everything which could be stopped was stopped. But the war began, too, a subtle process of local erosion. The county map was part of the national subconscious: the counties and even parts of some of them had their own dialects, their own special institutions and authorities, their Quarter Sessions and Assizes, not to mention convivial Societies for the Apprehension of Felons and the organisation of cricket. Motor transport had moved people about more in the latest ten years than ever before. Now the army deliberately mixed up the personnel of the county regiments. Direction of civilian labour often moved people far from the homes of their ancestors; so did the wholesale requisitioning of property some of which, such as at Lulworth Cove, has never been returned; so did the evacuation of children and refugees from the threatened or burning cities. The spirit and atmosphere of localism was kept alive mainly by the elderly, whose concern in the war effort was either voluntary or connected with agriculture.

At the same time the feeling that 'we were all in it together' made the local authorities into agents for the local civilian policies of the war-waging government, and happy to be. Where they did work required by war policy the government paid. Where local authorities had to do things which arose out of wartime exigencies, there was some government fund to back them up, and a promise of future indemnity if in the heat of the moment somebody overstepped the mark.

Nobody can, in the context of that war, reasonably criticise these developments, but they were pregnant with future effects. The ability of a council to project the collective personality of its area was weakened by the disappearance of much of that personality. The habit of agency connected the authorities in the public mind with Whitehall: they seemed to be local representatives of the centre rather than protectors of the locality against the centre: 'their men' not 'our men'. Concomitantly there came an elevation in the status of the paid and permanent official at the expense of the councillor: the latter, in fact acquired some of the character of an official, for elections were frowned upon, and the councillors became self-perpetuating and dangerously familiar with the wartime system. Thus the notion took root that local authorities had no justification save the utilitarian function of running public services in accordance with government wishes.

When, with Stalingrad and Alamein, it looked as if the tide was turning, men began to think about the Better World for which, it was to be assumed, they were fighting. Local government was not exempt from these speculations which, in 1942, took practical shape in discussions between four local authority associations about the future. The government in due course set up for local government the Boundary Commission (1945) and the Manpower Committee (1949) but meanwhile it was necessary to 'get on with the job'. The enormous schools programme launched by the Education Act of 1944, and the great regulatory powers for town and country planning created in 1948, were conferred or imposed upon a system in whose permanence nobody now believed. There was not merely a backlog of capital investment, but a policy, in real terms, of increasing it. Housing, highways, rural water and rural sewerage (at least that lesson had been learned) became objects of urgent government solicitude.

The financial situation was immensely complicated by confusion in the rating system through bombing, rent control, the low level of wartime business activity, the changeover from war-like to peaceful industries, combined with obsolete valuations. Debt was created at a phenomenal speed and at rising rates of interest. In 1944 outstanding local government loans amounted to £1,711m and average rates on new advances were 3¼ per cent. In 1954 the figures were £3,888m and 4 per cent. 'To reduce pressure on the rates', the local authorities were benevolently drowned in government grants, which, of course, encouraged further capital adventure. In 1964 the figures were £8,645m and 5¾ per cent; in 1974 £21,800m and 11⅜ per cent. In the single following year, when interest rose to 12½ per cent, the debt rose by twice as much as the total debts outstanding from the century before 1954.

The reports of the Local Government Manpower Committee are unfortunately forgotten, but the Boundary Commission discovered that it could not do its job without some authority over finance and functions. It suggested that its own powers should be enlarged in these directions. The Labour Government, through Aneurin Bevan, thought otherwise. In 1949 it wound up the Commission: and, as already mentioned, the list of local boundary extension Acts grew longer and longer.

The decision was not really surprising. The centralised welfare machinery which had grown up during the war was to be used in peace. Central direction, the method of victory, was the method of the time. There was no room for municipal generating stations, gas works and hospitals if such things were to be provided nationally. Local government could wait. It did not need to be much better if other agencies were to do the work.

The system of *ad hoc* government grants may have got essential things done, but it sapped the sense of responsibility of sometimes timid councillors. Moreover it was now said that somebody would suffer injustice if services of a uniform standard were not available everywhere. The central government had become a locally active and financially dominant partner. The Local Government Act, 1948, consecrated most (but not all) of the New Jerusalem. National policies thrust duties upon local authorities, for which the national treasury should pay: hence a general subvention. Standardisation required equalisation of resources by way of grants based on a formula which took into account differing resources and problems. Special matters such as housing and road building required specific finance.

These arrangements meant that the councillors were elected by one body of people to spend money, most of which came from another. Since World War II the public, bemused by ratepayers' propaganda, has never realised how much of the ordinary taxpayers' money has gone into local government. In 1975 it was two-thirds of all the money spent by local authorities.

'Local government' meanwhile was turning into a technical term meaning only that part of local administration carried on through elected local councils. The central government was quietly building up three types of local organ not locally responsible at all. There had always been the Post Office, the oldest nationalised industry, but as government nationalised others, there grew up local sub-managements and offices for them: for gas, for electricity, for coal, for railways, buses, and canals. In the process some (mostly urban) authorities lost utilities which they had pioneered and cherished. Then the various welfare

98

services such as pensions, national health and hospitals passed under the control of Whitehall (again depriving some authorities), which promptly spawned another new set of local organisations and offices. And finally there were the *ad hoc* authorities such as Drainage Boards.

This gave serious concern. It was said that local authorities were losing functions because they were too numerous and therefore too small and weak, but that if they were fewer and larger, something might be regained. This was, essentially, a professional argument, for professionalism was advancing everywhere. The permanently high level of taxation discouraged the volunteer. Until 1938 only Middlesex, Hertfordshire and Lancashire had had salaried chairmen of Quarter Sessions: by the 1950s only a very few counties had not, and in 1948 councillors were given extensive allowances at the ratepayers' expense. It is not clear how far the contention was self-interested: chief officers were strongly influential in the local authority associations, especially the Urban District Councils and their pay depended on population. On the other hand the Local Government Act of 1958 set up a reforming machinery, based upon proposals made by four of the associations; its operations were hedged about with safeguards so strong that in England outside the great conurbations only Shropshire, the Fenland Counties and Torbay were effectively reviewed in ten years. In Wales, apart from minor details, nothing was done at all.

Though it had no Scots equivalent, the 1958 Act kept the pot boiling until a Labour Government decided in the interests of standardisation and economy to abolish the distinction between urban and rural administration, and set up the Redcliffe-Maud Commission to find ways of doing it. In 1969 it accepted the general view of the Association of Municipal Corporations that, with parish councils as representative thickening, the best type of local government would be a system of uniform city regions. The public and the counties revolted: and anyway the uneven distribution of cities made the principle technically inapplicable. The Conservatives agreed that reform was necessary, but not in the manner of Redcliffe-Maud. When the electors put them into power they had to pass something else. The upshot shows how little they were influenced by the local authority associations: the operation was dominated by the chronic shortage of time between general elections. Urban and rural were indeed combined: county boroughs with counties, municipal boroughs and urban districts with rural districts. The principle of the Scottish reforms was the same but the new larger units were called 'regions'. The county map was partly redrawn in England. In Wales and Scotland the sweep was complete. Altogether 425 district replaced 1,722 town and country authorities. Where the urban units were really villages, this did not matter, but in a kingdom with an urban majority of 3 to 1 the countryside suddenly found itself represented in councils dominated by townsmen. The reform nearly coincided with the British entry into the Common Market and was followed by the economic recession. Just as agriculture had its price support system turned inside out, the postwar era of official rural investment suddenly slowed down, within a framework now dominated for the first time by party doctrinaires.

Water, sewerage and the health services were now taken out of the local government complex which they had created, and committed to yet more *ad hoc* authorities: so much for the theory that bigger authorities would have greater responsibilities. In truth local democracy was considered an obstructive nuisance; over 15,000 seats and 5,000 aldermanries were abolished. The intimate representation of the small man was left to a body of parish councils (renamed 'community councils' in Wales for no known reason). It was fortunate that these, under the impetus of their own association, had gained competence and confidence in the previous twenty years. It was, by contrast, unfortunate that only in Wales were impartial arrangements made for reviewing their geography.

These reforms came to fruition in 1974 and 1975, but they had matured over the years against a background of declining rural services. British Railways had been closing branch lines since Lord Beeching's notorious report in 1963. Now rural station closures and service changes began to cut the rest off from the hinterland. They even tried, in 1966, till stopped by public protest, to send travellers from Huntingdon twenty miles north to Peterborough to catch non-stop expresses back through Huntingdon to London. The buses were becoming unreliable, or disappeared, or failed to connect. Village post offices were hard pressed to stay open. For a moment it seemed that, with the internal combustion engine, there might have to be a return to the personal self reliance of an earlier doctrinal era. The oil sheikhs, however, ended that particular dream.

The planning policies and migration since 1944 had, meanwhile, altered the pattern of rural settlement. The population of the countryside rose, except in certain difficult areas, at twice the rate of the cities, but the numbers engaged in agriculture fell by 80 per cent. The rural populace was no longer primarily and patiently concerned with organic, growing things; its avocation had become mainly the impatient multiplication of the inert. A countryside inhabited by townsmen was taking shape. They wanted to make the villages in their own town image with concrete lampstandards and all.

They were much assisted by the accidents of history: the planners realised that it was cheaper to extend an existing sub-structure: to add, say, a bit to an existing gas main, than to start from scratch. From this economical principle was born the 'key village', that happy place which was to burgeon, while others less fortunate would stagnate or die. As far back as 1955 it was noticed that villages had a 'watershed population' (at that time about 750). Those above it tended to grow, those below to decline.

The key village concept was a planner's surrender to the past. Its counterpart was the New Town, a vast place for which enough government funds would be found to start from scratch. The 28 new towns elaborated since World War II invaded great tracts of rural territory and starved many villages of development capital. Yet agriculture is the most important industry in the world without which the world will die. To withdraw the settlements from the land is to make cultivable land increasingly dependent upon oil-driven prairie ideas. Perhaps, the oil sheikhs may change the planners' minds again, and the revival of the shire horse (already in experiment) may revive the hamlet too.

CHAPTER 7

TOURISM

Reg Hookway

EAST OF BIDEFORD, where I lived, is a rolling countryside of wooded coombes and high hedges, of small fields and little villages. We went there from the town, a friend and I, most winter weekends. 'Buller' Newcombe, our countryside mentor, guided us in following the Stevenstone Hunt. He always knew where the fox would run. We saw it more often than the stalwart farmers who made up the Hunt and were frequently in at the kill. We, townsfolk, went into a countryman's world. Not many of us went there from Bideford, and visitors from other places were rare occurrences. If someone was staying at a local big house, then it was a subject to be talked about. Nobody stayed on George Ford's farm or Bert Harris's, nor in the pubs or cottages. In the early 1930s not many cars were to be seen on those country lanes, even in summer.

Our summer-time weekend world was different. We went westward, across the bridge, to the coast: that marvellous arc stretching from the Torridge estuary to the wild cliffs towards Clovelly and Hartland Point. From April to the end of September this was our playground. We had the sand-hills at the far end of Northam Burrows; the wide sweeps of beach at low tide; the million pools on the wave-cut rock platform that extends westward from Westward Ho! and the Kipling Tors, where Rudyard roamed as a schoolboy. And always at hand was the sea, and the surf which we could ride from our early years; unless what Kingsley called 'the everlasting thunder of the Atlantic surge' was so loud that we knew it to be too dangerous for us.

We did not have this summer playground to ourselves. There were strangers about. They came for golf, and to swim and surf. The hotels were busy. At Westward Ho!, the Golden Bay Hotel stood in its acres of lawn above the cliffs. I have no idea if it was ever profitable but it certainly represented a bold act of faith on the part of its Victorian or Edwardian investors. The building is now a complex of holiday flats and the acres of lawn have been covered to a high density with holiday chalets. Perhaps 50 people stay there now to every one who came to enjoy the luxury of a big hotel. Most of them came by train. My father was licensee of the Swan Inn at the end of the bridge at Bideford; between the river and the railway station. We were very conscious of the 'season'. The number of trains was increased and what seemed to me to be crowds of people used the little station, pouring out of the trains with masses of luggage into a jostling and bustling frenzy of taxis and buses. Or we would watch them waiting to return to strange-sounding places. And what a day it was when a Campbell's steamer came up-river, and the trippers swamped the quay, so many of them with melodious Welsh voices.

It was a special occasion when a young 'masher' of a relative came in a car. In 1931 there were about a million cars on the roads, and no doubt the forward thinkers could see a time when more people would come by car to Bideford than would come by train. But I doubt if any of them foresaw that within 40 years no one would arrive by passenger train.

These were localised impressions of a child who knew little of the existing large British domestic holiday industry. Capital had poured into the building-up of the holiday resorts round our coast and inland. They were served by the then huge railway network.

I can find no estimate of the number of people who took holidays away from home in 1931; no national tourist board then assembled such information. The large resorts knew how many came by train but not by car. There were very wide disparities of wealth within our society and it was the 'better off' who went on holiday. There was much cheap labour to provide a service; we were just coming out of the

Depression. The majority of holiday-makers stayed at hotels or boarding houses; a few would take a house and might bring their servant, or a service would be provided. Self-catering holidays were not common, and it was mainly the younger few who walked, canoed or camped. But the effect of the car was to be seen. 'Bed and breakfast' signs were appearing and many a little place did 'Teas with Hovis'. We took in visitors; there was room for six. They had bed, a gargantuan breakfast and sometimes a gargantuan dinner as well; we thought it marvellous extra money for very little work. There was a visitors book, with names and places to stir the imagination. We even began to have 'regulars'. One was a member of Parliament from Birmingham. I confess that I knew little about Parliament then, but I doubt if it ever addressed its attention to a subject as politically insignificant as holiday-making. We in the coastal holiday area of north Devon were beginning to appreciate its benefits, nevertheless. It brought a supplement to a hard-earned living; it provided employment when unemployment was rife, and it was something to talk about. Yes, tourism was good. Farmers could sell cream for teas, and cottagers their spare vegetables. Others saw a chance to sell petrol, or acquired a bus or taxi for hire. People were buying a little extra furniture or having some building work done. The so-called 'multiplier effect' of tourist spending was beginning to reach the less frequented coastal countryside.

Except for the few who sought fishing, riding or rough shooting, or the even smaller number who had acquired a cottage as a second home, the visitor made little impact on the countryside of north Devon away from the coast. It was different in attractive country round the bigger cities, to which cars and buses were bringing increasing numbers of day visitors and the weekend holiday-makers. It was different, too, around the resorts. The car made it easier to explore the surrounding country-side. The holiday-makers who were travelling by bus and car also brought business along the road, to the inns and village shops, and even to the farms selling fresh eggs or fruit. The car was opening up country which was not accessible by rail. And the cars were followed by the charabancs, taking people of all age groups and of all types on the noisy, beer-swilling—or polite, tea with scones—holiday outing. Thus all the inter-relationships, the movement and supply systems, the seasonal employment patterns and the different types of entrepreneurs, which together make tourism, were spreading their tentacles through the countryside.

Up to the beginning of the war the number of holiday-makers steadily increased, as more secured holidays with pay. So did the use of the car: there were two million in 1939. There were other new features. A Mr Butlin had opened his first holiday camp in 1933, and realised quite quickly that there was a large demand for a low cost, gregarious 'give 'em entertainment', holiday package. These were the years when the middle class were erecting holiday homes on previously undeveloped stretches of remote coastline, in places like Cornwall and Norfolk. With more cars, more people were holiday-making in tents: primitive contraptions compared to the brightly coloured, modern, light-weight aluminium-framed, water-proofed nylon creations. Here and there too, just a few people were using railway coaches or old buses, or even boats, put on little-visited land near a convenient beach. Caravans, either touring or static, were rarely seen, and they too were very different from those we see today.

Few people had holidays during the war. There was no spare petrol and tourism was virtually at a standstill. The coastal resorts of our eastern and southern seaboards were subject to occasional air attack, and there, and elsewhere, hotels and boarding houses were taken over to accommodate servicemen. But many young servicemen and women, and the young women who had joined the Land Army, had a close, if unexpected, experience of rural life. The years of the war were years of rapidly widening experience for a great number of people.

It took a little time for tourism to catch up and pass its pre-war levels, but by the early 1950s visitors were coming in hordes at the peak of the season. They came in regular trains and special trains, and, when petrol rationing ceased, in cars, buses and lorries. They came on bicycle and on foot. What is more, a very high proportion of them came without a reservation in advance. The number of touring holidays increased very rapidly. It was as much an attitude of mind as availability of money and transport. In July, in August and particularly over the Bank Holiday spell, the story was everywhere the same, a crowded moving chaos. At district and county council level, officials accepted this with a sort of resignation. Those who had to cope, such as the police, simply did their best.

I was back in Devon and closely involved with this intriguing activity, as Research Officer in the new County Planning Department of Devon County Council. We needed economic and social data for the County Development Plan. We had to process the deluge of applications for permission to develop land and buildings to meet growing demands. It seemed that everybody wanted to own a camp site. On the edge of the established holiday resorts this was understandable. But they also wanted sites at places without shops, without cafés, without cinemas, with no police, ambulance or fire services, no sewer and sometimes no piped water or telephone. Some were even ignoring the Town and Country Planning Act and opening new sites without permission. Others claimed that they had established, by virtue of the siting in a field of that railway coach or old bus before the war, an indisputable right to cover twenty acres with caravans or tents at thirty to the acre!

Planners were particularly concerned with three things. The first was to find out what was happening in the caravanning and camping boom. To help this we flew along the coastline in a light aircraft, taking photographs of every collection of tents and caravans we could see. Secondly, we tried to get a measure of the holiday season. We knew the pattern, of course: the quiet winter months, save at Christmas when there was a return flow of native sons and daughters; the first minor peak at Easter, the next at Whitsun and then, in July and August, the great surge before the quick drop back in mid-September to winter levels. But what were the dimensions? How many people were coming? What was the size of the peak? What did it mean in terms of employment or income? Thirdly, what was involved for the public authority if the trends of recent years continued? What sort of roads would we need? Could we meet the demands for water? What about the sewers? And so on.

Working with the help of officers of the British Travel and Holidays Association, established in 1950 to promote international and national tourism, we tried many ways to measure the changing volume of visitors. We studied the sales of newspapers, postage stamps and virtually anything for which we could find figures giving seasonal variations. In the end we concluded that the best and most readily available guide was a chart of the weekly takings at public conveniences. This indicated the changing number of visitors, and the number was the key to so many other questions.

It was becoming clear that tourism was bringing into the county of Devon more revenue each year than its great farming industry; that tourism was the base for a great many full-time and part-time enterprises, and was providing substantial employment, in a growth industry. This was disturbing advice to county councillors whose long-standing

(*Above*) As the Forestry Commission spread its trees across the countryside so various expedients were tried to house their workers. This is Dalby village in Allerston Forest, north Yorkshire. (*Below*) Forestry machinery became larger and more sophisticated; the OSA 705 Processor working in pine at Thetford, Norfolk, debarks, cross-cuts and stacks the timber

(Above) Hunting has kept its strength as a rural sport; this meet of the West Kent Hunt was at Hever Castle in 1955. *(Below)* Horse shows and gymkhanas have also grown tremendously in numbers and popularity and often without the social standing; notice the modest cars and the new small houses at this event. Hunting was once a male preserve; now half the riders at any meet and the majority at a gymkhana or horse show, are likely to be women

creed had been that their primary concern must always be for the county's primary industry, agriculture!

Devon's main attraction was, and still is, its coast. But increasingly, and in particular on dull or damp days, people began to drive from the resort towns and the new colonies of caravans and chalets which had transformed the character of so many small coastal settlements, into the deeper countryside. If the weather forecast was poor the owner of the country pub or knick-knack shop, or the warden of the church or any place to which the curious might be attracted, took special notice. Almost any attraction was worth advertising, and it still is. Old buildings never experienced such pressure of human feet in their heyday. Natural features such as caves and viewpoints, and man-made attractions—model villages and zoos of varying types—could be the basis for business. The towns, the villages and in particular the roads seemed congested. And when a very rural Devon farmer pulling a trailer of hay came face to face with a very urban holiday-maker pulling a very large caravan in a very narrow, sunken Devon lane, the sparks would readily fly.

Increased use of footpaths, wear on areas of common land or heath, and crowding at natural beauty spots were beginning to cause concern. On a summer weekend, rather than go to the crowded coast, we might take our children to the banks of the Dart at Hexworthy on Dartmoor. There they, and a handful of other children and parents, could play amongst the boulders and on the sand shingle at this lovely place. But more people came. It was decided that they needed 'facilities', and these attracted more people. Is this not true for a thousand places in Cornwall and Cumberland and Cardigan, in Denbigh and Dorset, and in the inland counties, too?

Throughout the 1950s and 60s there was a steady growth in the number of people taking holidays away from home, and in facilities and services for them; particularly in self-catering accommodation, relatively cheap and suited to the mobile family tourist. Not unconnected with tourism was the growth of retired settlement in holiday areas. The mums and dads who retired provided a holiday base for the sons and daughters. And the mums and dads themselves, with leisure time to use, added to the tourist pressures on the day trips. Many holidays are spent with relatives.

Countryside of great beauty, now designated as national parks and areas of outstanding natural beauty, attracted large numbers of day visitors, even to places without a history of visitors. How could this in-flow of humanity be absorbed without destroying beauty and peace? How do you conserve rare wildlife when thousands are curious to see it? A designation for protection was almost an act of publicity! It was as though the very last inner secret areas of the countryside were under assault.

By 1971 I had worked for six years in Norfolk, served the National Parks Commission which in 1968 was made the Countryside Commission and, after a brief spell away, returned as its Director. In 1931 I was a schoolboy in a depressed coastal holiday area; in 1951 a local government official concerned with the boom in tourism in a holiday county. In 1971, my duties were wider but associated with holiday-making still.

What a change over those forty years! The million cars have increased to nearly twelve million. The whole scale and patterns of tourism are different, and the extent of government involvement as well. Holiday-making is part of the way of life of a very large proportion of the population. Government is concerned, not only indirectly because of taxation from leisure motoring, equipment and catering, but because the holiday industry is of national and international economic importance, and a source of considerable employment. More public bodies have been set up to promote tourism. The old British Travel and Holidays Association is now the British Tourist Authority, mainly concerned with international affairs. England, Wales and Scotland each have a National Tourist Board, and in England there are regional tourist boards as well.

None will dispute that tourism is an important element of the economy of much of our British countryside. Farm tourism is promoted as an appropriate enterprise for the farmer. The trade of many country towns and villages depends on the tourist inflow, at weekends throughout the year or during the main season. Many big houses are now country clubs or hotels. Many country inns have a sophistication beyond the dreams of the publican in the small town pub in which I lived. They are stocked with the liquid beverages of the world, not just beer and cider and a 'drop of short'! They gleam with brasses which never graced a horse. They are warm and 'plushy', with a 'juke box' or piped 'musak'. Many specialist restaurants have been opened, and it would be intriguing to know the number of shops selling antiques in rural Britain.

Whilst substantial areas of working countryside remain where tourism has made little impact there is an extreme which, verges on fantasy. Many of our stately homes are now pleasure grounds with visitors counted by the hundreds of thousands, and in a few places by the million, each year. The visitor may take a wildlife safari in his car and have a real lion jump on it and give him the fright, or the thrill, of a lifetime; and probably a substantial bill for a respray too. He may ride in fancy boats on ducal lakes or in fancy carriages down tree-lined drives. Children may use their energies in an 'adventure' playground; and for the adults there are fairgrounds and displays of—well, of almost anything one cares to think of. The display may be garnished with a battery of audio-visual equipment to 'enrich the experience'. It may be of old cars, of traction engines, of trams, of clothing, of guns and so on. The ingenuity seems boundless. Agriculture may be interpreted through displays of rare breeds of farm animals, or even of the working pro-cesses of a modern farm. Very few Britons have ever been in a milking parlour, or watched a sheep sheared, or held a chicken, or sat in the seat of a combine harvester. These things represent a new experience.

Are we interpreting our history when hundreds of us have a medieval banquet with 'Elizabethan' serving wenches and guitar-playing min-strels? Or when fewer of us dine with His Lordship off the exquisite Sèvres, or the gold plate? Or is this sheer escapism?

Public authorities are cautious about involvement in the colourful side of tourism, but are becoming increasingly concerned with the con-servation of the rural heritage. As well as old buildings, there are the collections of old machinery, centres of industrial archaeology, and folk and craft museums to interest us in our past. In some national parks, in new visitor centres, the visitor is told how we get food and timber from our countryside and about the farmers, the foresters and conservationists who care for it.

The voluntary conservation movement is worth special mention. Huge numbers of holiday-makers, either as members or paying visitors, get great delight from the properties of the National Trust. Others, with a more specialist interest in wildlife, enjoy the properties of the County Naturalists Trusts, or the RSPB. Still more are occupied with old rail-ways, canals, industrial plant and whatsoever.

In 1951, the British Travel and Holiday Association estimated that a little over half the people of Britain took an annual holiday away from home: something like 25 million in Britain and 1·5 million abroad. In 1961 the figure had risen to about 30 million in Britain and 4 million abroad, nearly two-thirds of us. Through the 1960s the numbers stayed much the same, but there were changes; the length of the main holiday slowly increased, and the number and length of additional holidays, the weekend break, increased rapidly. Thus the total volume of domestic holiday-making has continued to grow. Furthermore, holiday visitors from abroad, 415,000 in 1951, had risen to over 4 million in 1971, and some of these were exploring our countryside. The pattern of holiday accommodation has also changed. Although hotels have done well from the additional holidays, the growth sectors have been in self-catering accommodation. The continual increase in the number of static caravans may have reached its peak but the amount of self-catering holiday accommodation has continued to increase. New investment is in the purpose-built chalet, or the conversion into holiday flats of old cottages, and the out-buildings of farms and stately homes.

Whilst the coastal belt remains the great place of attraction for the British holiday-maker, much of this new self-catering accommodation is located inland. The boom in touring caravanning and in tented camping continues in coastal and country areas. Membership of the Caravan Club has increased from 11,000 in 1950 to 138,000 in 1973; of the Camping Club from 13,800 in 1950 to 144,500 in 1973. Their members can move on a motorway and main road system quite beyond the imagination of the motoring holiday-maker in 1931.

What of the future? Those of us concerned with policies related to the enjoyment of the countryside believe that if we have more affluence and more leisure, or more leisure without more affluence, there will be a substantially increased use of the countryside by holiday-makers.

A few years ago, speaking provocatively about tourism and the countryside at a conference organised by the British Tourist Authority, I advanced three comments I had heard in the few months preceding the conference. The first was 'Tourism is a destroyer of beauty and countryside'. It attracts people from elsewhere. It promotes the development of more roads, more hotels, pubs and restaurants, camp sites and petrol stations, and car parks. It creates more demands for water and sewerage. It produces litter. The second was 'Tourism is an exploiter of the resources of the countryside'. It exploits the attractions of nature, and those created by farmers and foresters. Its heavy demands for development, for a short season of use, necessitates heavy public authority expenditure for which the new development is inadequately rated. The third was 'Tourism is commercially selfish'. It creates an employment pattern which is seasonal and unbalanced. It is only concerned with profits, most of which go back to the towns. One conservationist demanded of me, 'Tell me one creative thing that any tourist board, agency, company or operator has done for the British countryside?'

In the heated debate which followed I argued that tourism is a mixed blessing, and to some people and to some countryside interests it is a curse. The changes it has brought to some rural areas can only be fully appreciated by those who can look back thirty or forty years. Even so, it is an effort to remember how markedly different things were.

But there are gains as well as losses. Tourism has contributed to maintaining the built fabric of the countryside. Without the demand for second homes many isolated cottages would have disappeared. Without tourism many parts of our small towns and villages, reflections of centuries of history, would have decayed. Tourism supplements the incomes of many who work the resources of the countryside. A lot of the money earned in the countryside by tourism does not stay in the countryside; but then a lot of the money earned in industry does not stay in the towns. With radio in virtually every home and television in most, it does not need tourism now to open the eyes of the countryman to the world beyond his physical horizons: indeed many countrymen are as avid tourists as townsfolk are.

Whether a blessing or a blight, tourism exists. It will continue to exist and that is the fact we must not ignore. I believe holiday-making is important to our physical and mental health as individuals and thus contributes to our social stability and national well-being. With so much instability in our great urban centres we need to have a special regard for this particular safety-valve. The wise countryman will extend a welcoming hand to tourism.

The wise countryman will also remember that we need more food, more timber and more water; that much in our countryside reflects a delicate balance between natural and human systems. Whatever the social merits of tourism there is no doubt that it can have a ruthless, greedy and selfish commercial side. Perhaps our control of development has not always been as effective as it might have been, but without it there is no doubt that there would have been much more destruction of rural beauty by tourist development. There is a need to question the argument that the growth of tourism is everywhere desirable. In many parts of the countryside much that is sensitive and beautiful would be destroyed by its unbridled increase. Planning and management must be designed to keep pressures in such areas at present levels. If more tourists are to enjoy them, then it should be by the spreading of the pressures over a wider season. We need to view with particular caution proposals to make it easier for vehicles to penetrate sensitive areas; for a tourist flood will surely follow. The national and regional tourist boards need to be brought fully into the systems of planning and managing the countryside so that their promotional arguments can be weighed in the balance with conservation arguments. We must make better decisions.

There is one final point to make. We live in an urban society. The affluence, from which our capacity to take holidays, have a tourist industry or practice conservation depends, is the surplus from the earnings of industry and commerce. No balanced view will discount the importance of producing food and timber from our land. But the interests and well-being of the countryside are dependent in many respects on sympathetic and favourable decisions from urban minds. Perhaps the greatest benefit of tourism to the countryside is that it has given a higher proportion of our urban population a care and concern for its conservation than at any time since we ceased to be a rural nation.

CHAPTER 8

FORESTRY

George Ryle

WORLD WAR I brought the biggest reaping of woods which Britain had ever seen. Softwoods primarily but hardwoods also: they all had their urgent war uses to counter the U-boat blockade. The Crown woods were comparatively diminutive in area so that, while providing their full share, huge sacrifices were demanded of private owners. Nor were they slow to respond. Even while the fields of Flanders were still a slough of mud and death, the Forestry Commission was conceived, to be born almost as soon as the war was over; and that is where our story begins. In 1927, when the first issue of *The Countryman* appeared, the Commission was getting well into its stride with a nucleus staff of trained foresters. Our set task was simple: to build up as big a reserve of growing wood as possible as quickly as possible. In its little way, but quite important in the deep country areas, this single policy provided valuable new jobs where the call for farm labourers was declining or had already ceased to exist.

Uncultivated lowland and rough hills came on the market in plenty. Though they were far cheaper to afforest than were the thousands of acres of those recently cut-over and now derelict woodlands, both were acquired with equal zeal. The Commission believed that the quickest progress would be secured by direct action. Though they instituted grant-aided schemes for a private sector which at that time was lacking in any real cohesion, they pressed these forward with rather less enthusiasm than they gave to their own pioneer task.

With steady acceleration as the baby woods became thickets spreading themselves over wider and wider landscapes, the face of parts of the countryside was changed, largely to something strange, even alien, on the British scene (or at any rate on the English and Welsh scene). It was at Eggesford in Devon that the Forestry Commission's first trees were planted, but a few months later in Norfolk and Suffolk the first really huge forest, Thetford Chase, was started on barren breckland. It now covers some 45,000 acres. On each side of the Scottish border, a little later, the 100,000-acre complex of Kielder, Wark, Falstone, Redesdale, Newcastleton and Wauchope with a few others close by became the biggest man-made forest in Europe and it was there that the ashes of Lord Robinson of Kielder and Adelaide, the great professional organiser of the Commission, were scattered over the highest viewpoint of this, his perpetual memorial. Eggesford, like most of the Devon forests, contains a wide mixture of trees, but Thetford Chase is almost wholly pine and the border forests are essentially spruce.

Development in Wales began too in 1920 in a rather more scattered way, but today the coalfield alone carries about sixty thousand acres of spruce, pine and larch with a scattering of other species, securing that my valley shall remain green despite the spoil tips and the pit-head gears. Now there is no county outside old Middlesex without new forests growing up or derelict ones being restored.

From early days broadleaf trees were planted, but on a very small scale. The demand for oak for ship building had of course dwindled to something totally insignificant although railway rolling stock was still made largely from native hardwoods. But softwoods were the great need.

The new land culture could not expand efficiently without woodmen who must learn fresh skills. Local labour was spread thinly so new blood had to be brought in. The original conception of just growing big woods had to be linked to a second policy of encouraging men and their families to settle nearby. Hence there developed the programme of building woodmen's holdings amongst the forests: houses each with their small range of outbuildings and a little land so that immigrant workers could grow roots of their own. These smallholdings became fiercely sought after both by country-bred folk from the neighbourhood and also by coalminers and others from the depressed heavy industrial regions. At first we had grave doubts about these last and we asked ourselves whether men and their families, brought up in the tightly knit communities of the mining valleys or the industrial north, would be able to acclimatise themselves to the remote hills and the hardships of out-door work in all weathers. We wondered whether mum would take to minding a few cows, pigs and poultry while dad was up in the plantations all day and the children were away down the lane in a strange village school. There were misfits, but the selection of tenants was always meticulous.

Visits were paid to the labour exchanges in Rhondda, Taf and Ebbw where interested miners were told of the hardships and isolation of life as a woodman. From the few who remained to hear more details a short list was drawn up. Then without prior appointment each was visited in his home. There were spotless shining homes and slovenly homes. There were back gardens replete with leeks, spuds and cabbages and there were others barren or full of junk. It was these homes and the attitudes of the wives who tended them which really decided us on our final selections. By and large these town workers quickly adapted themselves to become the same good countrymen which, in all probability, their forebears had been a mere two or three generations earlier.

In the years of economic turmoil between 1918 and 1939 the call to stop spending money on the long-term forestry gamble was effectively countered by the demand to keep men on the land and to help unemployment problems by speeding up afforestation and to settle more families into woodmen's holdings. The biggest such demand came in 1936 when the Forestry Commission was given funds for vastly increased plans for hundreds of new holdings. They even began to provide hutted encampments for re-training unemployed miners. This acceleration was just getting well under way when the march of Hitler across Europe changed everything.

After only twenty years, war again demanded immediate action and Britain changed from being almost totally dependent upon imports for her timber needs to being nearly self-supporting. Such a *bouleversement* was achieved only by huge and often totally uneconomic harvesting of the woods. The Forestry Commission's plantations were too young to be of significant use: again it was the private properties on which the call was made. For six years we had to keep the coal mines supplied with their pit timbers; the railways with goods wagons and permanent way sleepers. There were calls from the fighting services, demands for patching up after bomb damage, and for packaging. Even the oak and beech branchwood was converted into forest-burned charcoal and sent off to the munition factories.

As in 1916, World War II was still at its height when a minuscule team of experts quietly designed a fresh forest policy for the post-war years. Again national security was to be the keystone: the Forestry Commission was to move in a much bigger way and private woodland owners, now under their own democratic organisation, were to be properly encouraged with long term assurances. The result has been dramatic. From 1919 to 1939 the state woods had grown from nothing to a little over 400,000 acres (which included the absorption of the Crown woods), in the next twenty-year period to 1959 they swelled to over 1,250,000 acres. Likewise in the private sector planting had averaged less than 6,000 acres a year before 1939, while in the corresponding period after 1939, including the difficult war years, it exceeded 13,000 acres a year. Now it has crept up to 59,000 acres and in its spread over fresh land begun to run neck and neck with the Commission.

Immediately after the war direct employment in the woods reached its peak. To cater for the needs of increased manpower and, hopefully, for the more gregarious tastes of the 1946–1955 newcomers, forest villages were born, twenty or more identical houses, each with its wee garden, in the heart of the young forest with jobs guaranteed for the breadwinners only. Maybe a hutted village hall-cum-schoolroom which could also be used as a church or chapel on Sundays would be added. It was too much like a garrison town, but lacking the highlights of such a town and even the excitement of sudden postings to other stations. The forest village scheme had a short and troubled life, but gradually the discontented folk drifted away and the others began to develop that comfortable mateyness which is the soul of any small remote hamlet, lacking only the mixed spices of ordinary village gossip because everyone was working for the same boss and everyone knew the amount of his neighbour's pay packet.

The 1950s gradually brought an end to the post-war scarcity of machines and this had a profound effect upon the social problems of the forests. Mechanical equipment of increasing sophistication has enabled more and heavier tasks to be done by fewer men and these men, now better paid—though still not well paid—were able to choose their own homes in the nearest village proper or market town, getting to work in their own jalopies or transported in trucks laid on by their employer.

The regular clunk of a pair of axemen followed by the smooth *wheet-wheet* of the two-man crosscut saw has been replaced by the high-pitched shriek of a single motor chain saw. The hauliers with their team of sweaty horses have given way to the diesel-engined tractor with its own pungent smell. But there is still the sudden silence when breakfast brew-up comes: the mixed woodsmoke and the aroma of sizzling bacon and eggs, the blackened billycan simmering in the ashes, remind us that woodmen still remain basically unaltered.

The smallholdings built between the two world wars fulfilled an invaluable need for a generation and a lot of them will continue to do so. The yearning of some folk to occupy their own little farm is strongly ingrained. These men too will always be the cream of the woods staff, regularly employed but able to enhance their standard of living by home-produced food. But with a falling resident force, some of the little holdings and many of the forest village houses became redundant. The oldest and poorest of the smallholdings, especially those converted from decaying hill farms, were demolished, to be lost under the rising canopy of a more consolidated forest. Other holdings and individual houses in the forest villages found a use as holiday or retirement cottages. Given a fresh lick of paint more varied than the olive greens and railway station browns beloved of the old establishment, with flowerbeds replacing the cabbage patches, they began to serve a new purpose in the social life of their districts. New people with new countryside interests came to broaden the horizons of the woodmen and their families.

The ageless managed forest is much more than just a mass of trees; it must also support its own human family with a wide range of abilities and skills which are constantly changing with the invention of new equipment.

Very much the same trend has occurred amongst the well tended, privately owned woods. Both have been fundamentally dependent on their own regular woodmen but both have looked for economies by employing outside contractors. Investment in much of the heaviest or most specialised equipment, whether for soil cultivation, road construction or harvesting, can be justified only where the size of the enterprise assures that it can be fully utilised. The Forestry Commission has found that, despite those crushing overheads which it seems must bedevil all nationalised industries, it is reaching the stage where its own direct operations are competing favourably with undertakings by trading contractors. Indeed it would be disgraceful if this were not so because in many cases it has been the Commission's own engineers who have produced the modern machines which the contractors have adopted for themselves. The trend for the Commission and some of the larger owners or consortia to be self reliant in this respect is healthy because the peripatetic contractor will never have the same interest in the woods as the steady man who soon comes to look upon them as his own forest.

About twenty years ago the government began to cast doubts upon the value of forests as living stores of raw material which might be desperately needed for any national emergency. They knew that forests were conserving a better rural economy in the marginal areas. They knew that on purely financial grounds the return from timber growing was less attractive than some industries. They knew that a number of large wood-consuming factories had recently sprung up and that others were on the drawing boards, all relying on an expanding home production of logs and all valuable import savers, maintaining work in urban areas of fragile employment. They even knew that, despite plenty of criticism, Britain's new forests were fast becoming popular recreational areas. It was the beginning of a decade or so of confused policy where strategy had been ignored, commercialism had lifted a timorous head and the 'pretty pretties', lacking any very clear interpretation, appealed to the urban political mind. For social reasons there was to be a strong swing of effort directed to Scotland, rather less to Wales and a virtual hibernation in England. For the private sector it was realised that financial aid must continue to be provided and with periodical upward reviews. Throughout western Europe, governments have accepted that production of staple goods from the soil—agricultural or timber—can only be secured by state aid in some way or another.

The sense of urgency had been smothered, but a rather havering progress continued right up to 1973. The economists in Whitehall became enchanted with calculations about net revenues neatly discounted for the length of the tree crop rotations and these calculations indicated the alleged benefits of early fellings to grab a quicker return on the investment. They indicated too a proper need for controlling early operational costs which could mount astronomically when compounded up to the time of harvesting. They skimmed rather more gaily over the need to control administrative overheads. They tended to over-simplify the problems and to ignore that the needs in the years to come would be for maximum yield of a highly graded range of products as well as other less tangible benefits. These economists had perhaps not read the report of the government committee of 1916 upon which the Forestry Commission had been created. It had said then that the direct profitability of afforestation:

> though much discussed in this country, is not from the national point of view the most important and that it has never been so regarded in countries where silviculture has been longest practised and is most valued. The direct gain or loss is relatively a small matter compared with the new values created—these values being expressed partly in terms of population and partly in terms of wealth. It is on such values that the strength of nations depends.

The understanding of this 1916 committee of the word 'wealth' clearly implied that any sound forest management must aim at conserving an optimum stock of growing trees capable of yielding a high out-turn, even if in working to that goal fairly long rotations were adopted. Combined with a regime of generous thinnings, that was the way to greatest productivity.

It was in 1974, but only after strong representations from the owners' organisations, that the government announced a policy covering both the Commission's functions and plans for the encouragement of the private sector, bringing together for the first time the importance of a wisely planned use of the land, steady employment, the sound development of the country's timber resources, the conservation of the environment and the provision of recreational facilities. Though the government expected, in exchange for continued financial help and tax concessions, that privately owned woods should join with the state forests in providing means for public enjoyment, this was widely accepted as a necessary ventilator for an increasingly urbanised population. There would be many difficulties to be ironed out. Where shooting values approached or mayhap even exceeded expectations from lumber sales, how could the tourist crowds be guided away from the best coverts? Where large expanses or small regenerated pockets were at their highest fire hazard stage of growth, could they be specifically and practically excluded from public access? Such problems need to be covered in the management plans. In effect there would be very few complete imbroglios so long as the difficulties were allowed to be settled on the ground by true foresters.

Then came 1975 and *slap!* Down came the Chancellor of the Exchequer with his wealth tax and his capital transfer tax intentions, utterly discouraging those who had invested in the productivity of their sylvan soils for future generations. Of course these taxes were not aimed specifically at woodland owners but their effect upon forestry could only be disastrous. Young crops would be neglected because their proprietors could see no future in the investment. There would be strong temptation to harvest other crops which, though already marketable, were still many years before their prime; certainly there would be a lamentable lack of incentive to re-stock the cut-over areas or to continue improvement projects on the unproductive scrubs. Only a few weeks earlier agreement had been reached on the need to expand and to make productive the million or more acres of still poorly managed woods, aiming for that five million acres of efficient forest which had been the target thirty years earlier. Only the next few years will tell how or if a faith in the future of the industry can be restored.

The Forestry Commission's entire preoccupation in 1919 was to build up a strategic reserve of timber. They were aware of dangers in continuous monocultures of conifers, especially of spruce whose shallow rooting habit and dense needle fall could cause a deterioration of the site. But much of the land was fit only for conifers. There was no reason to expect that pioneer fir crops would bring about other than a beneficial change, which they have done especially since deep mechanical cultivation became the standard pre-planting practice.

There was already a little experience of Sitka spruce, a native of western America, being a very fast grower of valuable timber and this quickly became one of the major trees to be used in hill planting, especially on the peaty lands and in high-rainfall zones. It steadily gained favour over the hardy but slower Norway spruce and it just as steadily gained the opprobrium of sections of the public who were alarmed not only at the size of the new plantations spreading across the hills but also at the speed with which they shot up to make an entirely strange greeny-blue landscape. The wide expanses of Scots pine and Corsican pine in the drier regions caused anxieties elsewhere, though the growing woods of the more graceful Douglas fir and the larches (western hemlock was then hardly being used) were hardly distasteful to anyone who could distinguish one tree from another—to many they were all conifers and therefore alien. Criticism was by no means universal: Scotland with its old softwood forestry tradition was happy and in such places as the Welsh coalfield and the neighbourhood of industrial towns forestry was welcomed. Alien too was the geometric conformation of the rides, copied remarkably blindly from some of our neighbours on the Continent.

A large proportion of the development was of course happening in the remote hinterland where very few people then travelled and therefore few complained. Change of land use was looked upon with alarm by some hill sheep farmers, but where sheep farming was steadily going to the wall, the arrival of 'the forestry' ready to pay cash for land, was not at all unwelcome.

The mounting criticism, voiced especially by the CPRE, resulted in rather closer attention to the fitness of the scene even though this was primarily confined to the edges alongside public roads and tended to look, as in fact it was, very artificial. Some foresters planted roadside belts of native deciduous broadleaf trees, some went in for the 'churchyard trees', cypresses and western cedar, some even planted pink flowering cherries. But the wiser ones scrutinised the lay of the land from all directions before softening the broad conifer acres by introducing other elements. It was a gradual process of self-education which should have been a lot quicker; but the urgency remained on the strategic needs. Landscaping took second place and anyhow the baby woods would take on quite a different air when they ripened towards timber size and when silvicultural thinning obliterated the neat planting lines.

Nor were the hardwoods being ignored. On suitable soils and sites, especially on the old scrubs and cut-over lands, oak, beech, some ash and others were regularly planted, either alone or mixed with conifer nursing trees which would be removed with the early thinnings. Private landowners did more of this than did the state. The Commission was adamant that they would not use hardwoods in places which they could see would only yield poor growth.

It was not until after World War II that serious action was taken to rationalise forest roads and rides. From 1939 till about 1950 it was almost impossible to get hold of heavy earth-moving equipment. The Services had first priority; then the ill fated ground nut scheme in Africa made heavy demands, and (main stumbling block) nearly all of the best machines had to be paid for in dollars. Meanwhile the early plantations of the 1920s and 1930s were in desperate need of thinning. Much was done, but all too slowly, by horse 'tushing' along unmade rides which had been laid out on the old geometric pattern; but as dozers, graders, excavators and other juggernauts gradually became more freely available so there began a majestic programme of properly surveyed road building. Between 1950 and 1960 3,685 miles of heavy load-carrying water-bound roads were constructed, often over difficult mountain terrain, across ravines and even over deep bogs—about ten times the mileage between London and Edinburgh—and from then onwards the work was pushed ahead steadily. The geometric era of rather useless rides gave way to properly contoured roads which, besides being useful, naturally fitted in with the sweep of the hills.

During this decade too, the private motor car and better industrial holidays created a very reasonable call for better recreational facilities and scope for field studies in the wild places. The Forestry Commission had foreseen that this would happen even before 1939 and had designated several huge areas as 'forest parks'. Within these they began to make high-class tourist camping and caravan grounds. The main function of these parks was to open up mountains above the tree-planting line, rather than to show off the deep forests, but they quickly became unexpectedly popular and gave most valuable guidance to the Forestry Commission and to the yet unborn National Parks body. Three of the forest parks were in Scotland, one in Wales and only one on the Welsh-English border of the Forest of Dean and Tintern. Later the Kielder Forest Park on the English-Scottish border was linked contemporaneously with the new Cheviot National Park. None was close to the main urban centres of England, though the New Forest (which is not classed as a forest park because of its peculiar pony and cattle interests controlled by the ancient Court of Verderers) has become the outstanding example of multiple land use for the people, the commoners' animals, the growing of timber and the safeguarding of a very varied wildlife; uses which are not at all easily compatible.

In the early days, access to the woods had certainly not been encouraged; sometimes it was pretty rigorously forbidden, mostly because of a fear of fire. Now the principle of 'open forests' was gradually encouraged at the discretion of the regional conservators and in the less fire hazardous places. The freedom of the woods was progressively encouraged, but it was and still is strongly felt that it must be a peaceful freedom, remote from the noise and fume and scurry of the motor car.

(*Above*) The Dartford Warbler, a characteristic bird of the southern heaths, in in Britain at the northern limit of its range. Its British habitat is now under considerable pressure. (*Below*) The white admiral, a woodland butterfly apparently on the increase in Britain

(*Above*) The developing consciousness of the scenic importance of rural settlements and open countryside has led to the formation of many amenity societies.
Advertising such as seen at Otford village, Kent, in 1938 is now rigorously
controlled. (*Below*) The Council for the Preservation of Rural England has played
a leading part in many battles; in the 1970s it successfully opposed proposals to
flood Farndale in the North Yorkshire Moors National Park to make a reservoir

People could bring their vehicles into parking places cunningly concealed just within the gateways, but from there on further exploring must be afoot. For those unable or unwilling to move far from their cars small picnic suntraps were often laid out nearby. There followed also the creation of forest trails and nature trails, way-marked in a subdued manner and often provided with explanatory leaflets to enable visitors to understand what the woods were doing for their own day-to-day needs and to look deeper into the natural history and scenery.

Thinning in the older crops proceeded apace. Until this early revenue-producing operation became subjected to rather artificial rules emanating from the top, most foresters and nearly all of the more progressive landowners evolved quite bold systems (after the French *éclaircie par le haut*) whereby the maincrop trees, to be allowed to grow on to maturity, would retain a strong upper crown formation and thus be encouraged to make vigorous diameter growth, yielding fat poles and finally large sawmill logs. This bold approach also gave an early change in the appearance of the plantations: the straight rows became completely blurred, more light was let in, any dense carpet of needles began to disintegrate and maybe a natural herbage or shrub layer crept in.

Now the use of the woodlands by visitors has grown to a torrent. From scores of skilfully planned camp and caravan sites, nearly all of which are for short tourist holidays from spring till autumn, the Commission is now advancing to groups of permanent chalets and even talking of woodland hotels (or is it motels?). That will need very careful watching because it could too easily urbanise what ought to be rigorously preserved as semi-wilderness: anyhow it is not forestry!

However, the State occupies less than half of British woodland and soon its own properties alone will hardly be able to cope with the need for public access. So private owners whose woodlands are subsidised from public funds or subject to tax concessions are being called upon to co-operate. It may never be desirable that all woods and forests shall become open for public uses, and there is probably little for anyone to fear. All that we must ask is that groups taking advantage of the concessions should become far more active in training their folk to respect what is thrown open for their pleasure and in taking positive steps to discipline those who perpetrate mischief or who behave carelessly.

Already the plantations formed in the year of *The Countryman*'s birth are being felled. If some think that they are being felled a decade or more too soon, that is because professional economists (who can look backwards with some clarity but can only look ahead through a glass darkly) have calculated that the best returns will be obtained through a policy of short rotation cut-and-come-again. With the Commission's fellings now running at some 7,400 acres a year, it would be hoped that deep thought will be given to the methods of such clearings and how best to ensure a second crop which will possibly have a higher yield capacity and will certainly conserve fertility. This second crop too should abolish the complaints about huge expanses of even-aged monocultures which had been inevitable in the first formation. There can be nothing more attractive than a mixed wood where the new thickets are growing up beside the mature timber and where the mid-aged ones being systematically thinned can be seen just across the pathway. Nor need the groups of the different ages be of such small size that transportation of the timber to the roadside would become unduly costly. What is important is that they should be irregular in conformation to merge with the topography (and so also with normal extraction methods) and have careful regard to the prevailing storm winds. Aesthetic fitness and the provision of optimum habitats for the forest denizens will then normally follow.

There is not yet very much evidence that felling and regeneration in the older state forests is being designed on other than large block plans so that after a few years of apparent devastation the second crop will again arise in extensive woods of unnaturally uniform age and height. Landscaping, even on such larger scale, appears to take pretty low priority beside the desire for quickest possible harvesting and great opportunities are being lost to develop fine silvicultural systems.

In recent years, there has been a response to the call of some environmentalists for broadleaf trees. Not only has the Commission decided that more oak and beech must be used in the southern counties, but it will give higher grants to private planters who follow suit. With the most careful selectivity this change of emphasis—which need not be the prerogative of the southern counties—will fill a long-felt wish. In the replacement of mature softwoods with hardwoods the opportunities for small-scale, irregular methods will be particularly attractive as well as being ecologically sound. The broadleaf trees will always develop to their best under conditions of moderate side shade and protection from the harsher elements.

We have only recently joined the European Economic Community, in total a big importer of wood from outside sources and, unless it pulls up its socks, these foreign imports will have to increase rapidly. There is so much wasteland within the EEC which could be made to grow good timber that the common agricultural policy, already in some confusion, must be broadened to become a common food and wood policy. This can only help to bring our own little island problem well outside little island party politics into something bigger and more stable.

Maybe the fast growth of our own wood-using factories, giving employment to both urban and rural workers and steadily easing our balance of payments, will be the strongest argument to favour a more progressive and stable policy but, as part of the EEC, this progress is the more likely to accelerate. During the last fifty years Britain has far outstripped any of her neighbours in new afforestation, though still remaining far behind them in the proportion of land surface devoted to forests. But these neighbours will teach us now the values in silviculture of second and later rotation crops: ecological values, amenity values and even productive values.

To repeat what was said in 1916: 'it is on such values that the strength of nations depends.'

CHAPTER 9

RECREATION

Victor Bonham-Carter

FIFTY YEARS AGO the old order of the countryside was still in the saddle, though slipping; and to many impartial observers collapse seemed only a matter of time. History however is peppered with false forecasts and, in terms of recreation, nothing is more striking than the way the countryside has come through—altered but very much alive.

As a youth in the 1930s I had had ideas of becoming a land agent in Wiltshire, then worked for a spell on *The Countryman* at Idbury, and ended up before the war with a town job and a cottage at Inkpen in west Berkshire. I played village cricket every Saturday in the summer, was a keen rambler, and went for long walking tours in the Lakes and in north and south Germany, where I had joined the pre-Nazi youth hostel association. My wife was an avid naturalist and an enthusiastic horse-woman, who had done a hard stint in a riding stable in Warwickshire. We had friends with large country houses, working farmers of different shades and grades, and many others who got by on the produce of a garden and very few pounds a week. We were able therefore, though young and inexperienced, to watch with interest and some insight the

130

rearguard action deployed by the rural hierarchy to preserve its traditional habits and amusements.

Field sports were still dominant. Hunting was both a privileged pastime and a common passion, defying class barriers outside the town, and it had a long history. Before the great Enclosures there was plenty of space; and even by 1850—when most of the open fields and many of the commons had disappeared—no tenant farmers and few others dared, or even wished, to oppose a sport in which almost everyone in a locality participated. A similar story might be told of the other two traditional field sports—shooting and fishing. Both began as forms of local foraging, pleasurable as pastimes, and continued—so long as game was abundant— more or less uncontrolled. Regulations, where they existed, were designed to protect rights of property rather than species; and casual poaching was widely winked at, except in times of scarcity and social unrest when gang warfare was waged between poachers and keepers. In general, until the late 1800s, most countrymen could and did shoot or trap game and catch fish, legally or illegally, and of course follow the hunt on horse or on foot. It was all part of the rural way of life.

By the twentieth century the whole country was divided up into hunting territories, ranging from the snob packs of the midland shires, financed by wealthy masters and their friends whose families had probably made their money in industry, to locally found packs in the hills of the west and north, run on a shoestring with a minimum of panoply and fuss. Even in the worst years of depression between the wars, cash was forthcoming for the 'wire' and 'poultry' funds, and most people tolerated some hunt damage as part of the price of the sport, freely allowing hounds and horses passage over their land. Fox was the principal quarry, red deer on Exmoor, fallow buck in the New Forest, hare and otter in particular localities.

Shooting also varied widely. At one end of the scale was the farmer who flushed out partridges from a field of roots, bagged a hare on a summer evening or netted rabbits in a hedge with a ferret. At the other end was the landowner who reared pheasants by the score, whose gamekeepers shot every predator as a pest, and who employed an army of beaters on shooting days to drive the game towards a line of guns. His aim was to provide large bags for weekend guests or for a syndicate which paid heavily for the privilege. A grouse moor or deer stalking in Scotland were important elements in the income of certain estates, which managed the land and preserved game for the purpose.

131

On the fashionable trout streams, such as the Itchen and the Test in Hampshire, and on salmon rivers in Scotland, the fishing rights were mostly in private hands and changed hands but rarely. The sport was carefully managed, as it still is today. Waters were stocked and 'gardened'; and fishing limited to a specific number of rods rented out at high prices each season. Visitors however could buy day tickets on stretches of water owned by clubs or local associations, or stay at an hotel which had fishing rights.

These three—hunting, shooting and fishing—were by their nature integral to rural life and society. They gave employment to breeders, keepers, vets, farriers, shops and suppliers of equipment, and represented a large business investment. They were supported by a lively press and bore a mystique all of their own. 'Do you hunt?' was the opening gambit in a tireless social routine, and the reply was rarely the one offered by Oscar Wilde, 'Only when I have lost something'. Hunting apart, it is hard now to recall that, as late as the 1930s, the horse was still the main motive power in farming, it took farmers and their wives to market, and even in large towns it played an important role, especially in the delivery of goods. In many families it was an over-riding passion. Children rode ponies till their late teens, riding and management were encouraged by pony clubs, rallies, competitions and the like—all as a prelude to adulthood and full devotion to horse use and ritual, though less organised, less professional than now, and quite distinct of course from the national industry of racing. As a cult, the horse permeated subjects more vital than recreation. For example, its importance long survived its usefulness in the army (and not only the British Army), and contributed to the failure to develop the tank for war, and all the disasters of 1940 and after.

Popular as they were, hunting and shooting were already under fire by 1939. The fact that their advocates regarded conservation simply in terms of rearing game for slaughter was already disturbing public opinion; but there were other more effective sources of criticism. One was the revival of farming which induced many farmers to plough up pasture and destroy scrub in order to restore heart to the land. Another was the outcry raised by ramblers, highlighted by mass trespass in 1932 in the Peak District, a dramatic symptom of the nationwide agitation for access to the countryside. Another was the growing opposition to 'blood sports' on ethical grounds. Lastly, colouring it all, was the widespread feeling that field sports were the preserve of a moneyed social class, that kept others off the land and enjoyed killing for its own sake.

Not a field sportsman myself, except very inadequately with a gun, I preferred some of the alternative amusements available in the village. Cricket, for example, wasted no time and brimmed with action. Two innings each side plus tea, all inside four hours, was a common occurrence. It was also the 'compleat' social leveller. No one wore 'whites' that I can remember, while classic stroke play was unwise owing to the irregularities of the pitch and the unpredictability of cowpats. Unless the batsman attacked the ball, it was likely to shatter his wicket or strike him in a sensitive part. It was all do–it–yourself, and we got to away matches by begging lifts in other people's cars. Football too was a self-sufficient enterprise, taken perhaps a touch more seriously, with the team being picked on Friday night in the back room of the Olive Branch. I had had enough football at school, but when working on *The Countryman* I used to play hockey for Bourton on the Water. An urban middle-class intrusion? Possibly—but our centre-half was one of the local auctioneers, often late for the start, because selling store cattle had taken longer than expected. These and other gregarious games were all part of the community of village life. Wives and 'birds' kept the score, brewed the tea, attended to wounds, and joined us in the annual dinners which they also made. Recreation at this level, like the summer fêtes at Whitsun and August bank holiday, was directly descended from the seasonal revels of the Middle Ages, before the reformers replaced them with more seemly sorts of celebration.

Survivors of these abounded of course, as they do today—cider wassailing, Shrovetide football, May Day hobby horses, Rogationtide bound-beating, harvest homes, mumming, dancing and singing. Even where they seemed rather self-conscious folk revivals, especially if watered down into evening classes or children's party pieces, they were salutary reminders of man's dependence upon nature. I used to think on these things often during the war, as did others, in long spells of boredom in uniform. What came out of it in my case was a plan, ultimately made possible with the help of many neighbours, by fund raisings and grant-aid, and by expert advice from bodies like the National Playing Fields Association, the National Council for Social Service, and Berkshire County Council, to buy land in the centre of the village and lay it out for football, cricket and a children's play space. Inkpen Playing Field, opened in 1946, was a good war memorial. I hope it is still there and in full use.

The war put an end to a lot of things, for the time being at any rate, but it also encouraged a great deal of re-thinking about the future, not least room in the countryside for mass recreation. Immediate post-war legislation laid the foundations: notably the National Parks and Access to the Countryside Act 1949, with ten parks designated 1950–55, extended at intervals since then by the development of forest, regional and country parks, the re-casting of rights-of-way, and the registration of commons. These moves made it possible to guide, if not wholly contain, the leisure explosion so ably identified and described by Michael Dower as the 'fourth wave'.

Broadly, the use of land for leisure in our time falls into two main categories. One is the enjoyment of the indigenous pleasures of the countryside, already outlined in their pre-war setting. The other is the growth of essentially urban recreations in rural areas.

Great efforts have been made over the past thirty years to train young people in the arts of citizenship through rural recreation. This is not a new idea, but the war so accelerated the pace of change that the situation today is barely recognisable. Had it not been so, the great growth in population and the compelling demand for equal opportunity might have destroyed society itself. As it is, despite everything that has gone wrong, society has survived; and for that we owe a heavy debt to all that has been done to create opportunities for youth.

The most important founded itself. Robert Baden-Powell, the soldier hero of Mafeking, wrote *Scouting for Boys*, advising youngsters to cultivate the manly virtues by playing out Kiplingesque frontier adventures in the open air. He offered his system of training to the Boy's Brigade but it was rejected. Boys themselves began forming patrols and demanded adult help, and the formation of the Scout movement was forced upon Baden-Powell. Girl Guides soon followed, and though World War I took away many of the leaders the movements survived to blossom in the 1920s. World membership now runs into millions with 600,000 Scouts and 800,000 Guides in Britain alone. In many ways they are urban organisations because that is where the children are, but much of the acceleration of the outdoor movement in the late 1920s and 1930s was a result of town children having learnt about the countryside from their Scout and Guide camps. Even short trousers, which the Scouts had made respectable wear for youngsters, became acceptable for the new race of country walkers.

Since World War II the Outward Bound movement has sprung out of the fertile mind of Kurt Hahn, head of Salem in Germany until expelled by the Nazis, and then of Gordonstoun where the Duke of Edinburgh and the Prince of Wales were at school. Hahn's dictum, 'It is wrong to coerce young people into opinions, but it is a duty to impel them into experiences', has found expression in six schools (one for girls) each with about a hundred students at a time, and located on the coast or close to mountains and wild country. The purpose is to build character and self-confidence through knowledge and experience of the country-side at first-hand. The concept has been followed in various forms and with varying degrees of success, in state and private schools and by youth organisations all over the country. It has been taken further still by the second scheme, the Duke of Edinburgh's Award, designed to catch the 'unclubbable young'; it has a strong countryside and adventure element and by April 1974 the number of entrants exceeded a million.

Exploring the countryside is older than the youth movements however. Railways first made it possible. The Commons, Open Space and Footpaths Preservation Society grew out of the battles to keep the commons round London from the enclosers and since 1865 has been the champion of access to the land. The bicycle took people out of the towns and the Cyclists' Touring Club (under another name) dates back to 1878. The invention of the safety bicycle in 1885, the pneumatic tyre, and even bloomers for ladies made the sport immensely popular and the CTC was an early developer of cheap country accommodation for the traveller. There were walkers as well and by 1905 there was a national Federation of Ramblers Clubs, formed into the Ramblers' Association in 1935 and now 32,000 strong. They too needed accommodation and the Youth Hostels Association, following the German model of 1914, was formed in Britain in 1930. Not reserved solely for young people, it ensures cheap beds all over the country in 160 or more hostels. Now it has 275,000 members and an annual overnight record round the two million mark.

The coming of the motor car after World War I made access to the country even more convenient, until 'a drive in the country' is now possibly the major recreation of the British. But car driving and motor cycling became a sport as well, and the 1920s saw country roads being used for rallies, trials, and treasure hunts; the roughest unmetalled roads sought out for hill climbs. The eighty motor clubs with about fifty members each of pre-1939 days has soared to the 800 clubs now recognised by the Royal Automobile Club, which issues 30,000 competition licences a year. The Auto-Cycle Union estimates that some 10,000 competitors take part in trials every year now. Since 1965 legislation has limited the use of public highways and the more dashing events take place off the roads. But motor cycle scrambles—'moto cross' in European English—in the field of an amenable farmer attracts some 6,000 competitors to over 500 events a year. If these are largely urban sports it is clear that for many village youngsters the motor-cycle and its associated fantasies is a powerful attraction and in many cases scrambles are rural events in setting, spectator and competitor. For many villages in summer too, there is banger racing in which 'jalopies', cars bound for the scrap heap, are stripped down and raced to destruction round a field. It is a poor man's sport with prize money of the order of £8 a race but, in 1975 one club alone raised nearly £6,000 for charity from gate money.

The amount of traffic which drove motor sports off the road—that and the disturbance the cars caused in quiet areas—also hit cycling. Membership of the CTC fell from 53,000 in 1951 to 18,000 in 1971, but by 1976 it was rising again and over 25,000.

All these recreations show a use of the countryside by urban and rural people alike. To some the qualities of the countryside are part of the pastime, for others they merely provide the space not available in towns. Of nothing is this more true than of the pop festivals where hordes of youngsters congregate for long weekends of endless popular music stridently amplified. The Thames Valley Police have had to cope with three 'free' festivals in Windsor Great Park and one at Watchfield near Swindon in 1975, as well as the Jazz Blues and Pop Festival each year at Reading since 1971 which charges £6 a head admission. There were 40,000 people on the Saturday of the 1975 event, adjudged by the police 'a very busy and well ordered gathering' with damage slight compared with an equivalent football match, but some drug-taking. At the smaller 'free festivals' the purpose was little to do with music; if anything it was social and political, a protest against the Establishment in favour of an 'alternative' anarchical society, characterised by drug-taking, nudity, communal copulation and physical dirt. Even so a police booklet (*The New Society*, Thames Valley Police, Kidlington, Oxfordshire, £1.50) says 'the majority of people who attend a free festival are predominantly but not exclusively young people attracted by the opportunity to "rough it" and escape the normal routines and pressures of life'.

These things are in the country if not of it. They reflect modern society. The older sports, cricket, football (and rugby football in some areas) still flourish. The cricketers now all have their 'whites' and the footballers elegant 'strips'; there are more leagues, more Sunday sport, and better playing fields and ancillary facilities. Many of these are due to the efforts of the Sports Council, a Government-sponsored body formed in 1965 that assumed the heaviest commitments of the Central Council for Physical Recreation (founded in 1935). It has given nearly £5 million to sports associations, helping to provide innumerable pitches and playing fields. There has also been great help from the National Playing Fields Association, which administers the King George V Foundation, established in 1936, for the same purpose. With this help village sports grounds have made remarkable strides from the rough fields that served in the 1920s.

Against the background of all these developments, the traditional recreations of the countryside, hunting, shooting and fishing, despite the loss of about 2m acres to building and forestry, and despite a host of other, largely urban, pressures, resulting in much less elbow room for these sports, continue to flourish—in some ways as never before. With the rise in cost of living, they have become more expensive; indeed expense is about the only effective way of controlling demand. To keep a horse at livery now costs about £20 a week, while shoeing runs into £6–£8 a set. Yet, though no longer a convenience, the horse is as high on its pedestal as ever, and supported by a high degree of professionalism.

The Pony Club, an international body with 320 branches in the UK, has an enthusiastic following of young people up to the age limit of 20, taking part in working rallies and gymkhanas, gaining efficiency certificates, attending lectures and film shows, and absorbing the whole gamut of equine lore. Where the Pony Club ends so to speak, its parent body, the British Horse Society, continues, sustaining in a score of ways the cult among adults.

Those who ride seem to divide into two categories—hunting and competitive riding. Hunting is a winter sport, and in essence the pattern is little different to what it was in the past. Apart from cost, it has suffered to some extent from intensive farming and the reluctance of business-conscious farmers to run the risk of damage to crops, animals and fences, however careful the riders may be. Moreover followers in cars often prove to be a serious nuisance on the roads. Another deterrent is the anti-hunting movement led by the League against Cruel Sports, which has been buying land in the West Country to deny access to hounds, and mounting activist campaigns in the field and in the press.

Far the strongest threat resides in proposals for legislation—the latest move being the Bill to stop hare coursing.

Those interested in competitive riding have an all-the-year-round programme to enjoy. The sport is fostered by numerous riding clubs and shows, while eventing at Badminton (dressage, cross-country, and showjumping) and the Horse of the Year Show at Olympia are among the highlights of this immensely popular form of recreation. Finally even the tyro who has never ridden before can now do so in comparative comfort and safety, thanks to the development of pony trekking. While the work horse has all but disappeared, interest in the riding horse has increased; but for reasons of cost and tradition it remains a predominantly middle-class pastime.

Shooting is expensive by any criterion, even if restricted to an evening stroll on the farm to bag a rabbit or reduce the appalling over-population of pigeons. A moderately priced 12-bore gun costs anything up to £500, imported at that, for a good English gun can command as much as £7,000 upwards new, with a 2½ years wait before delivery; and the trade is booming. Even cartridges cost £60 plus per 1,000. Clay pigeon shooting, with clays at 3p each and no game to sell or give to friends at the end of the day is not cheap, yet the sport is growing fast, with 5,000 individual members in 1975 and 350 clubs affiliated to the Clay Pigeon Shooting Association.

Game shooting costs most. To take one example. A friend of mine shared a gun in a syndicate of ten. That means he shoots at weekends, probably six days' sport between October and February. For this he pays £425 a year (exclusive of cartridges, travel and other incidentals) and is allowed to keep one brace per shoot for himself. The birds—pheasant and duck—are reared on a 1,200-acre estate in the home counties, where the landowner employs one gamekeeper and two assistants; beaters are paid £4 a day each. Charges vary of course in different parts of the country. In another syndicate in the South-West you pay £1,000 a season, but on fashionable shoots much more than that. On one estate, where the 19-gun syndicate is reserved, it is said, for visiting diplomats and Japanese business men, the charge is £600 a day. One can only conclude that, even at that price, the cost of rearing 10,000 pheasants and 5,000 partridges, plus the services of a dozen gamekeepers, has to be subsidised by the Foreign Office or the export department of the Department of Industry and Trade! All this smacks too much of the era before World War I, when birds were slaughtered by the thousand, hedges allowed to grow out, spinneys unthinned, and broad grass verges left round the fields: in short, sport at the expense of husbandry. In fact the situation has fundamentally changed since 1945. Shooting people have come to realise that their future depends on a far wider understanding of the management, not only of game, but of wild life at large.

The Game Conservancy set up in 1970 employs a staff of research scientists who investigate game problems, and an advisory staff who pass on information to the shooting public. The Wildfowlers Association of Great Britain and Ireland (WAGBI) has nearly 300 affiliated clubs and 13,000 acres of reserves. In all it controls 'excessive' shooting over 350,000 acres of varying types of land—marshes, moorland, quarries, forestry and farmland. While shooting remains their prime object, these bodies are concerned with the whole range of bird breeding, rearing, recording, and habitat protection; and, like the hunting fraternity, they claim that—thanks to culling and control—their sport ensures that species survive which, if left to nature and the normal predatory instincts of man, would die out. The Game Conservancy estimates that game shooting turns over about £60 million a year, taking into account lettings, wages, rates, tourism, sales of goods, and taxation.

Fishing stands alone in that it excites virtually no opposition among animal lovers. It appeals to a very large and socially varied public, and its interests are powerfully protected by the Anglers' Co-operative Association which campaigns with great success against pollution. As a result, many rivers, ruined for years by industrial effluent, are now clean and stocked with fish. A recent survey revealed that over 3 million people went fishing in England and Wales in the year ending May 1970 —2 million in inland waters, 1 million in sea waters. Coarse fishing is now the biggest leisure industry of all, weekly anglers totalling about twice the average attendance at Saturday afternoon professional football matches. Their prey is mainly pike, roach and perch (but other species too), caught mostly in slow-moving rivers, canals, lakes, pits and reservoirs in the Midlands and the North. By tradition it is mainly a working-class sport, strongly competitive. Equipment is expensive. A professional coarse angler can easily spend £500 on his tackle, though fishing tickets are cheap. Match-fishing is widely organised, and much money changes hands in the form of prizes, side-bets, and the like. For the non-competitive coarse fisher, tackle is relatively inexpensive. £50 will set him up comfortably, while day tickets from hotels and shops cost very little, though the river stretches so rented are often liable to be overfished. The casual visitor can often do better by travelling to a reservoir. Many new ones have been built since the war, they are well stocked, and there has been a welcome change in the attitude towards recreational use of such waters. Excellent sport can be had for as little as £1 to £5 per day, and no prior booking is necessary. Salmon fishing in Scotland varies enormously. To take one example from a friend who writes, 'I belong to a syndicate of 5 on a beat on the middle part of the river Tay in Perthshire in September. The current charge is £400 for one week, which allows 5 rods to fish, costs being shared accordingly. We hope to catch 25 salmon in the week, which are equally shared irrespective of who actually catches them. On more prolific beats lower down the river, one can pay £700–£800 and catch perhaps 100 fish.' As usual, rates for foreign business men are considerably higher!

One last word, one last look at the last half-century since *The Countryman* was launched in 1927: the pattern of recreation in the countryside, indigenous or imported, has changed most in that due to higher wages and the general re-distribution of wealth the number of people taking part has enormously increased. With that change has gone much of the social distinction between sports and sportsmen, in spite of cost, even in the traditional and socially conscious sports. In the face of such change, the greatest wonder of all has been the ability of the countryside to absorb the increase, without serious defacement, and without losing the essence of recreation, of whatever kind, and however regarded.

CHAPTER 10

WILDLIFE

Bruce Campbell

CHANGES in the numbers and range of plants and animals are governed by natural causes or by the direct and indirect effects of human action. Over as short a time as fifty years and in an island so small and heavily populated as Britain, we tend to think that man will be the dominant agent of change. But this is not necessarily so: climatic influences can operate quite quickly and in the most violent forms—great gales and floods. Some autumns, thousands of sea-birds may be blown miles inland, as in the famous 'wreck' of Leach's petrels in 1952. Adverse winds may wipe out migratory flights of insects or small birds and thus affect their status; an abnormal high tide may destroy the whole output of a tern colony on an exposed beach. Hard winters take a more lasting toll; a Martian visiting Britain after the cold spell of early 1963 might be forgiven for thinking that the goldcrest was one of our rarest birds. But the plants and animals native to a country are adapted to weather short-term disasters and their numbers usually recover in a few years, unless other factors complicate the situation.

More important are the long-term climatic effects caused by what meteorologists still subjectively call periods of amelioration and deterioration, lasting several or many decades. When *The Countryman* first appeared, Britain was enjoying a relatively favourable spell, which is supposed to have come to an end around 1950. Since then there have been indications of deterioration: a shorter growing period for plants, snow lying longer on the Scottish hills, but the expected three hard winters out of ten have not materialised. There are a number of species, birds like the Dartford warbler and bearded tit, living in Britain on the northern edge of their range which could be exterminated by a run of cold winters. On the other hand, several birds whose mobility enables them to respond quickly to quite small climatic shifts have in recent years increased in numbers or started to breed in northern Scotland.

There have also been one or two examples of colonisation from the south in response, apparently, to long-term climatic changes in Eurasia and, although Britain is an island, it can be penetrated not only by winged creatures and by marine plants and animals, but by the propagules of land plants carried by winds, waves or birds. But almost all the contributors to the symposium on the changing flora and fauna of Britain, organised by the Systematics Association at Leicester University in 1973, agreed that man has been by far the most important agent of change since records were kept. Man, unless he is trying to exterminate a pest or to collect specimens of rarities, does not usually operate against individual species; his effect is on habitats in general.

Small as Britain is, there are many places in which the view in 1977 will not be very different from that in 1927; routes can be planned, even in southern England, through countryside which still gives the 'this is where we came in' feeling, where fields are still small and hedges tall, scrubwoods sprawl over hillsides and valley bottoms flood in winter. But over the past half century huge acreages have seen either a complete change in their land-use or profound modifications in character.

Over the fifty years, what may broadly be called urban encroachment has taken thousands of acres annually, for houses, factories, power stations, roads, airports and defence installations. Such transformations are seldom reversible and involve almost complete displacement of the existing wildlife, though by no means the elimination of all plants and animals. On the other hand, the fetish for tidiness which affects the urban mind means that gardens and road verges are sprayed with biocides, and that parks become exercises in making trees, flowers and grass look as artificial as possible. Such areas enjoyed some respite during the war of

National Parks were
designated to protect their
natural beauty and afford
outdoor exercise: *(Right)*
Dovedale, in the Peak
National Park with its
solitary hiker represents the
ideal. *(Below)* The scene
below in the Goyt Valley,
also in the Peak Park, shows
the pressure of people; it has
now been made a traffic-
free zone on summer week-
ends

(Above) Traffic produces a major problem particularly with large lorries in the narrow streets of old villages. *(Below)* Industry brings many intrusions, the latest coming with North Sea oil. This oil platform is under construction at Nigg Bay, on Cromarty Firth

1939–45, but one of the first peace-time reactions was to expel nature with the more efficient modern equivalent of the pitchfork.

All the same, parks and gardens can become important refuges, chiefly for plants and invertebrate animals: Denis and Jennifer Owen have recently shown the remarkable number of insect species, including some of national rarity, that live in or pass through a small suburban garden in the city of Leicester. As well as cultivated areas, there are numerous odd spots, even in heavily built-up zones, where some native flora persists and gives protection to animals. One remarkable transient phenomenon during our period was the proliferation of native and escaped plants on the bombed sites of British cities: the buddleia bushes attracted butterflies and the ruins provided nest-sites for the black red-start, a bird which has now become a permanent breeding species in small numbers in the London area and elsewhere, finding our huge new coastal power stations one alternative habitat.

A by-product of development which can favour wildlife is the creation and then dereliction of quarries and gravel pits. Recently worked quarries with sunny aspects have their own climates, reminiscent almost of southern Europe, favourable for a rich flora and for butterflies and other winged insects. One large quarry near Oxford has banks bright with hundreds of spotted orchids, its floor covered with shiny new motor cars awaiting transit. More important are the worked-out gravel diggings, most prominent in the Thames Valley from Gloucestershire to the outskirts of London, but now found along many river systems as far north as County Durham. To naturalists their spread is associated with that of the little ringed plover, one of the southern invaders mentioned earlier. It first nested in England in 1938; by 1973 it had bred in over 30 English counties, in Scotland and North Wales. This small wader is most at home on areas of bare gravel with easy access to shallow water which, if unpolluted, is quickly colonised by aquatic vegetation and makes an excellent habitat for dragonflies. Unfortunately many shallow pits fill up at once when pumping ceases, and recreations like angling, sailing and water-skiing prefer deep waters. These can be valuable wildfowl refuges in winter if not disturbed too much and if compromises can be arranged between the various interests.

One famous man-made habitat on the urban edge has almost disappeared since the war, the old-style sewage farm whose sludge beds with their teeming invertebrate life attracted migrant birds at the seasons of passage. The shallow worked-out gravel pit can to some extent replace them; so can the shores of a reservoir like Chew Valley Lake in Somerset, which has become in about twenty years one of the most valuable ornithological sites in the south-west, as well as a most popular angling resource. Large reservoirs in southern Britain and lochs deepened by hydro-electric schemes in the Scottish Highlands have been notable post-war developments. But, after an initial boost to the growth of their trout due to increased feed from the 'drowned' perimeters, the lochs, most of them oligotrophic (lacking in nutrients), have not made a significant contribution to wildlife resources.

Although not so immediately apparent, the effects of the farming revolution of the past thirty years are potentially even more far-reaching than those of urban encroachment on the countryside. Farmland of some type still occupies between 80 and 90 per cent of Britain's land and is therefore the main home of our wildlife. It was really chance that the land-use pattern of the field and hedgerow checkerboard, with its nodes at farmhouses, stackyards, hamlets, small woods, ponds and marshes that came to dominate most of lowland Britain and much of the uplands after the enclosures, should have proved to be the ideal environment for a teeming wildlife. Hedgerows are attenuated strips of woodland, with maximum edge effect—the ecologist's prescription for diversity—sunny and sheltered sides where insects can fly, and thick cover for sallies out into the fields. In the ponds, streams and neglected ditches, not only frogs, toads and newts spawned in peace but a rich invertebrate life flourished. The spinneys and shelter belts were fortresses for larger birds and mammals; the stackyards were winter refuges for smaller species: seed-eating birds and harvest mice hiding in the ricks before threshing. These communities were probably at their best in the first decade of our period, when the farming recession discouraged tidiness and drainage schemes. The hand of the game preserver, though heavy on birds of prey, stoats and weasels, was heavy also on trespassers, and the motorised invasion of the countryside had hardly begun.

Although grazing pressure by farm animals on the downlands was reduced, a multitude of rabbits took on the job and saw to it that the brilliant flora of cropped chalk and limestone grassland and the rarities of the East Anglian brecks had a suitable milieu.

The war in 1939 ended this relatively happy state of affairs, sweeping away leisurely methods of farming and old practices like hedging and ditching by hand. Ancient grassland was ploughed up and reseeded, the combine harvester sounded the knell of the rickyard and demanded

146

bigger fields with their concomitant of fewer hedgerows. On top of this, in 1953–4 myxomatosis, presumed to have been imported by man, emptied the countryside of rabbits, reaching even to remote islands and to the basaltic 'greens' of the West Highlands that once seemed to move with their grey-brown forms.

The hedgerow problem has attracted much attention because it has both historical and biological implications, and because the removal of hedges is so obvious and can be statistically assessed. But it is misleading to suggest that Britain would lose a single species of plant or animal if all hedgerows were eliminated. Their inhabitants are orginally from the woodlands and many of them have also adapted to life in gardens, parks and scrubland. What must result, of course, is a diminution in the numbers of certain species. Birds, relatively easily studied and sensitive indicators of change, furnish examples. At the end of the war the chaffinch was generally regarded as the most abundant British land-bird. It cannot claim that position today and has been overhauled by the blackbird, which is as much at home in central London as on the moorland edge in Shetland, whereas the hawthorn hedge suits the chaffinch particularly. If the various schemes under consideration for planting up and 'enriching' odd corners of farmland to compensate for the loss of hedges should be realised, then the effect of their disappearance on our wildlife will be much reduced. At the same time, replacement of traditional hedging by mechanical cutting for a broad-based triangular section is a fairly acceptable substitute.

In the past decade the arrival of a virulent strain of the Dutch elm disease fungus (weaker strains have been present for the past fifty years) has further complicated the situation, especially in those counties where the elm has not only been the common standard tree but, by means of sucker shoots, has provided much of the hedgerow. Since it seems established that the new strain entered the country in imported timber, man, as with myxomatosis, is once more to blame.

The impact of Dutch elm disease was immediately apparent; but ten to fifteen years earlier the side effects of widespread use of chemicals on the land had crept up on us. It is easy with hindsight to wonder why no one realised that spraying crops with herbicides and pesticides, especially those of known persistence, and the dressing of seed corn, would start a chain reaction beginning with the soil fauna and leading to the larger predatory mammals and birds; or that residues would seep into water bodies and effect aquatic life as well. The ornithologists may claim to have sounded the alarm first in Britain as 'incidents' mounted up in 1960–1, the worst mortalities being in areas of high farming where the preparations were most used. Not only did small seed-eating birds perish—the changed numerical status of the chaffinch dates from this time—but the birds of prey, at the end of the food-chain, suffered even more severely. The analysis of bodies for chemical residues was both expensive and difficult, so it was greatly to the credit of the Nature Conservancy that it set up a unit under N. W. Moore to study the problem. His persistent advocacy on a series of committees of enquiry was backed by the research of D. A. Ratcliffe and others who showed, most notably for the peregrine falcon, how the persistent organochlorine chemicals worked: some birds died, some failed to breed; others laid thin-shelled eggs that broke easily. The evidence, at first circumstantial, later received experimental backing in the United States.

The initial breakthrough was the agreement by farmers to observe a voluntary ban on most uses of the persistent organochlorines, while manufacturers adopted a more responsible attitude in the testing of new formulations. The bird-eating sparrowhawk, once the gamekeeper's *bête noire*, was given special protection after it had virtually vanished from eastern England, and has now made a good recovery. Once the use of dieldrin in sheep dips was stopped, the golden eagle, which feeds partly on sheep carrion, showed improved breeding success. Writing in 1976, it is possible to claim that the situation is under control and that no vertebrate animal is under threat from farm chemicals.

The apparently beneficial application of fertilisers was even less suspect at first than the use of toxic chemicals; but gradually, as algal 'blooms' built up in water systems, it was realised that large residues were draining into ditches, rivers and lakes and causing 'eutrophication'. Too much oxygen was absorbed from the water and this operated against other forms of life. The waters of Loch Leven, a shallow basin into which small burns drain from agricultural land, became so clouded with algae that its famous trout had difficulty in seeing the lures presented to them. The problem remains; so does the result of aerial spraying of fertilisers on rough pastures, the flora of which soon suffers a detrimental change.

The advent of farm chemicals was something new to the British scene; land drainage is only the continuation a process that has been going on ever since man became a cultivator, and the really massive operations took place before our period. But in the past half-century farmers have recognised that the ponds which they had hitherto regarded as necessary for their stock were potential disease hazards, and so was marshland, the home of the snail host of the liver fluke. They also needed more land, and modern machinery now made it economic to drain hitherto intransigent areas. Urban encroachment also meant that old village ponds became polluted and derelict and it was easier to eliminate them than clean them up. In the past few years the attitude has changed and the Save the Village Pond campaign met with a remarkable response. It remains to be seen whether European Wetlands Year 1976 will succeed in safeguarding the marshes, bogs and lakes on which so many species, from diatoms to herons, depend. The Norfolk Broads, an historic area of ancient turf cuttings and Britain's most important wetland for wildlife, now threatened by intensive pressure from pleasure boats, pose a problem of special difficulty.

Even before man seriously attacked the low-lying lakes, meres and fens, he had largely destroyed the native forests by felling, burning and grazing. With the remarkable progress of state and private forestry since 1920, we now have some $4\frac{3}{4}$ million acres of afforested land. Most of it is covered by introduced conifers, often colonised by plants and animals which may themselves be alien: a rhododendron understorey may harbour rabbits, pheasants and several kinds of deer, while grey squirrels (though they prefer the hardwoods) climb the larches above. Most of the post-war planting has been on acid moorland of minimum agricultural value and with a limited wildlife, but conifers have also replaced native scrub of greater interest. For much of our period a policy of 'coniferisation' extended also to the old oak woods of the Crown forests, our richest land habitat for wildlife. This has now been halted, part of a generally more human face to state forestry. Although our forest area is by European standards very small, it has proved vital as a sanctuary, and the relatively prosperous position today of wild cat, pine marten and polecat, let alone a virtual explosion of deer, owes much to the Forestry Commission's black blanket of spruces.

Afforestation has therefore been the main factor affecting moorland over the past fifty years, though a good deal as far north as Orkney has been ploughed, sown to grass and turned into reasonable grazing. Enormous areas in the north of England and the Scottish Highlands remain as grouse moors and deer forests. The red deer is at a peak of numbers, perhaps around 200,000, and attempts have been made to 'farm' it

as the best crop for the worst land; the reindeer, established experiment-
ally in Strathspey and the Cairngorm Hills, shows no signs of becoming
a competitor.

Moorland's southern counterpart, heathland, especially that dominated by bell heather and dwarf gorse, is the habitat least appreciated
and most at risk in Britain. It occurs only in north-west Europe and the
British examples in Dorset and the New Forest are the best that survive.
But its unique quality has no commercial value and it is fair game for
forester, builder, ball-clay extractor, soldier and industrialist. Even those
areas which are common land or otherwise enjoy some protection are
near large centres of population and suffer constant erosion from
humanity. Yet these heaths are the home of many species on the northern
limit of their range and their destruction will impoverish our wildlife
for ever.

The impact of the townsman on the countryside is heaviest for wildlife
along roadsides and at the margins of fresh and salt water where there
are vulnerable plant and animal communities. Human pressure can be
regarded as a form of pollution, since it contributes to the spread of
noxious residues and effluents over the whole environment. The past few
years have seen limited gains, in the restrictions on farm chemicals and
the cleaning up of some rivers, notably the Thames, to which the re-
appearance of a salmon in 1974 was international news. But the general
menace remains, as sea and land are both contaminated. There have been
unexplained deaths of sea-birds and only too explicable mortality such
as that following the wreck of the giant oil-tanker *Torrey Canyon* in
1967. Smaller incidents occur continually, as a lorry crashes and spills its
load of poison or the wrong tap is turned and effluent pours into a
fishing river. The risks inherent in a technological society are many; so
far our wildlife has survived remarkably but there is no guarantee that
the luck will hold.

One conclusion reached by the biologists at Leicester in 1973 was that
increased interest, both professional and amateur, in many groups of
lower plants and animals made it impossible to assess changes in their
status. Many new species (193 beetles since 1945) have been identified
and the apparent decline of others may only mean that their known
haunts have not been visited or that the worker who made them his
special study is no longer active. A recent enquiry by the British
Naturalists' Association into the distribution of the glow-worm showed
that while it had declined in many southern areas, its range extended

much farther north than expected due to an improved cover of observers.

Among the lower plants, lichens are extremely successful colonists of bare substrates. Most lichens are sensitive to air pollution, especially by sulphur dioxide, but two bark-haunting species are extremely resistant and have increased dramatically. Other fairly tough lichens from a natural stone habitat have colonised various man-made surfaces. Asbestos cement has now a characteristic lichen flora, whose bright orange-yellows relieve many an otherwise dreary urban scene. But on the whole, man's recent activities have meant a great impoverishment of lichens, especially by the removal of old trees in the interests of 'woodland management'. By comparison, climatic influences have been unimportant. The position of the mosses is much as for the lichens: decreases due to various massive modern developments.

The situation of our higher plants has been thoroughly investigated by the Botanical Society of the British Isles, whose *Atlas of the British Flora* (1962) not only set up a base line for continuing research but established the 10km square as the unit for distribution studies of British wildlife. Some changes in recent years appear to be natural, due to seed dispersal by wind or along shores. Most changes, however, are due to man; a good example is the beautiful fritillary or snakeshead, a spring flower of valley meadows, highly susceptible to ploughing. Before 1930 it was known in over a hundred 10km squares; by 1973 it was down to 24 stations in 12 squares (see map). Excessive picking and uprooting have also played a part in this and other decreases of attractive rarities; the classic example is the lady's slipper orchid, reduced from 24 stations to one, which has to be guarded throughout the flowering season.

Many species, on the other hand, profit by disturbed conditions due to man-made upheavals. A number of these are successful aliens, and the map shows the spread of the small, prostrate New Zealand willowherb. Less hardy aliens are associated with warm rubbish dumps and provide excitement for botanists in urban areas. Rubbish dumps, incidentally, are one of the reasons why thousands of gulls have come to winter inland. Roadside verges have been a bone of contention between conservationists and highway authorities for the past quarter century, which has seen the arrival of the motorway. Minor roads verges may be the last refuge of plants banished from reseeded fields. Now that spraying has generally been discontinued, the economic climate of 1976 suggests that

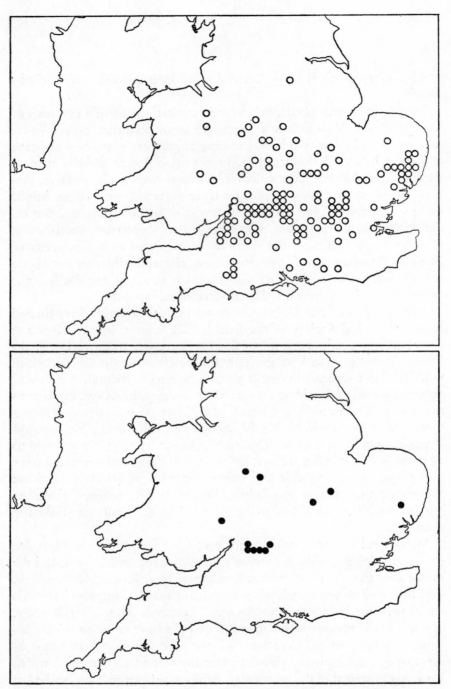

Changes in the distribution of the fritillary or snakeshead *Fritillaria melea-gris*; the upper map shows pre-1970 records (open circles), the lower map shows post-1970 records (solid circles). From *The Changing Flora and Fauna of Britain* with acknowledgements to Academic Press, London and New York.

cutting will be minimised too and it will be up to the naturalists to manage selected stretches of verge.

Verges also house the food plants of a variety of insects and may be very important to butterflies like the marbled white whose larvae feed on grasses. For some ten to fifteen years of our period there have been jeremiads about the decline of our butterflies and moths. Some authorities believe that, for once, climatic fluctuations are the principal cause; others blame man's activities. Certainly the large blue, inhabitant of old pastures, and the large tortoiseshell are on the edge of extinction. Others appear to be holding their own and even increasing; the woodland white admiral is one of these. But it is likely that nature reserves will become the main reservoirs for a number of the scarcer species.

Apart from natural immigrants like the clouded yellow, we have no alien butterflies; but successful, usually accidental, introductions occur in most other insect groups. One of the most remarkable is *Cis bilamellatus*, 'a small, cylindrical sexually dimorphic brown beetle' studied by Dr Kitty Southern. First discovered near West Wickham in Kent, in 1884, it was believed to be an entirely new species, living in the dead, dry, fruiting bodies of the birch-bracket fungus. Later it was shown to be identical with an Australian beetle, and must have entered the country in material for a herbarium. By 1933 it was still confined to south-eastern England; then a major spread began (see map). Did the host fungus become commoner or has increasing interest in entomology led to more identifications?

Most of the vertebrate animals have now been mapped by naturalists working in collaboration with the Biological Records Centre at Monk's Wood near Huntingdon. Fish show little evidence of natural changes: they are restricted by pollution, or spread by deliberate transference and the stocking of new waters, so that it is now impossible to define the original distribution of most species. Several aliens have become established, and the native vendace of Lochmaben, one of the freshwater whitefish, seem to be extinct. Our few amphibians and reptiles have been subject to a general decline over the past thirty years, during which man's activities—spraying, draining breeding places, collecting—have once again done their worst. The natterjack toad, always local, has suffered a disastrous contraction of range and both smooth snake and sand lizard are being given urgent conservation first-aid. All three are inhabitants of the southern heathlands whose whole fate is in jeopardy.

In contrast, birds are in an almost euphoric situation. Having wea-

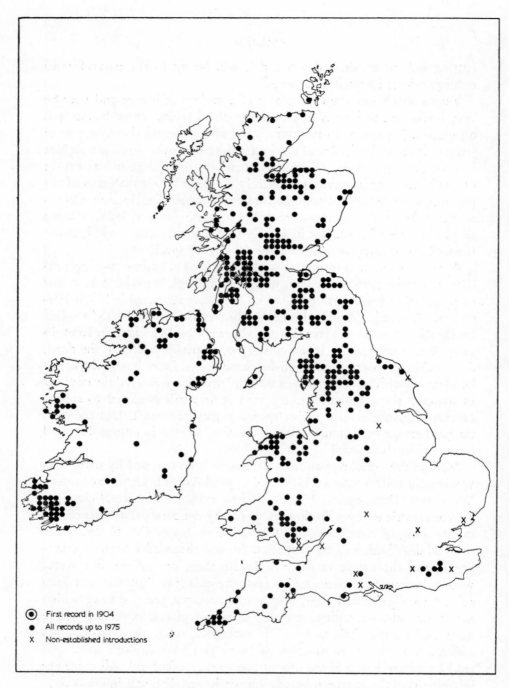

Spread of the New Zealand willowherb *Epilobium brunnescens* (formerly *E. pendunculare* or *E. nerterioides*). With acknowledgements to the Biological Records Centre.

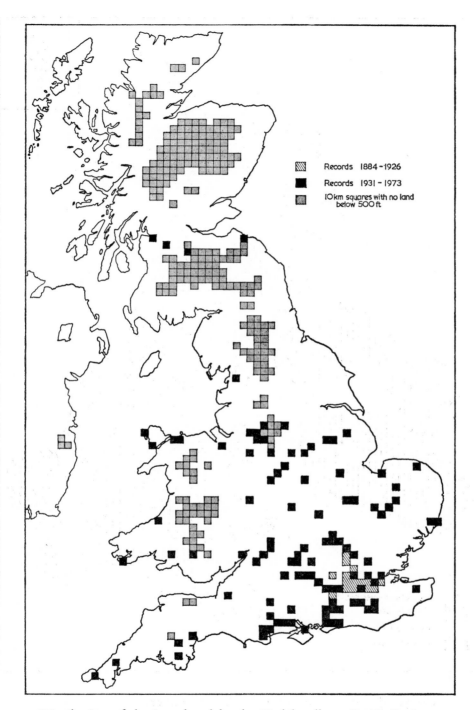

Records 1884-1926

Records 1931-1973

10km squares with no land
below 500 ft

Distribution of the introduced beetle *Cis bilamellatus*. By K. Paviour-Smith, with unpublished data from D. B. Atty, R. A. Crowson, J. H. Flint, C. Johnson and J. R. Lidster.

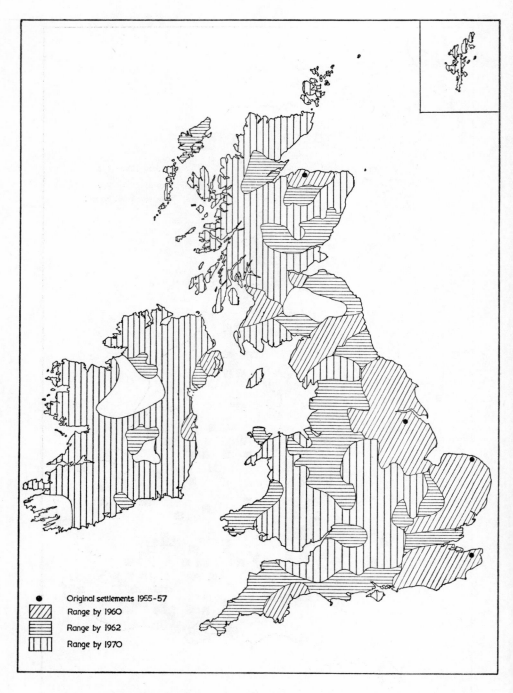

Original settlements 1955-57
Range by 1960
Range by 1962
Range by 1970

The spread of the collared dove. By Robert Hudson.

thered the era of toxic chemicals, defended by the more effective of our motley protection laws, supported by the strong and rapidly growing Royal Society for the Protection of Birds, and profiting by a network of nature reserves, there were more species nesting in Britain in 1975 than ever before in recorded times. Possibly in response to climatic deterioration there has been in recent years an infiltration of 'northerners', of which the snowy owl is the most spectacular, but 'southern elements' such as Cetti's and Savi's warblers and the golden oriole are also doing well. Since 1955 the collared dove from the south-east has run riot across Britain and Ireland, apparently exploiting an empty commensal niche (see map). Our famous sea-bird colonies have been assessed and, while numbers are not as astronomic as once believed, several species—we have more than half the world's North Atlantic gannets—continue to increase, and the decline of others, like the puffin and guillemot, may have slowed down. In the sphere of pure rarities, the past 25 years have seen an astonishing tally of transatlantic vagrants added to the British list, many of them landing in the favoured Isles of Scilly to be welcomed by a reception committee of bird watchers.

The British mammal list has achieved two new bats in recent years, the grey long-eared and the mouse-eared, formerly a vagrant and, with the greater horse-shoe bat, smooth snake, sand lizard, large blue butterfly and 21 rare flowers, given special protection under an Act of 1975. None of the native carnivores are considered to be in danger—foxes and badgers are now suburbanites—though many people would like to see the otter protected and even the reintroduction of the wolf, the last native mammal to be lost. But aliens continue to be established, some like the various kinds of deer more or less welcome, others in the pest category like American mink and coypu. Coastal fishermen would include as a pest our internationally rarest mammal, the grey seal, of which more than half the world's population breeds in British and Irish waters; for almost all our period a debate as to its merits and management has continued.

Finally, two land mammals which epitomise British attitudes to wildlife. In 1930 the red squirrel had recovered from a mysterious crash at the beginning of the century, and introduction of the North American grey squirrel had virtually ceased. The maps show the situation between the two in 1974. Their inter-relationship remains something of a mystery; but the grey squirrel is primarily at home in broadleaved woodland, to the forester's distress, the red squirrel in conifers. Before

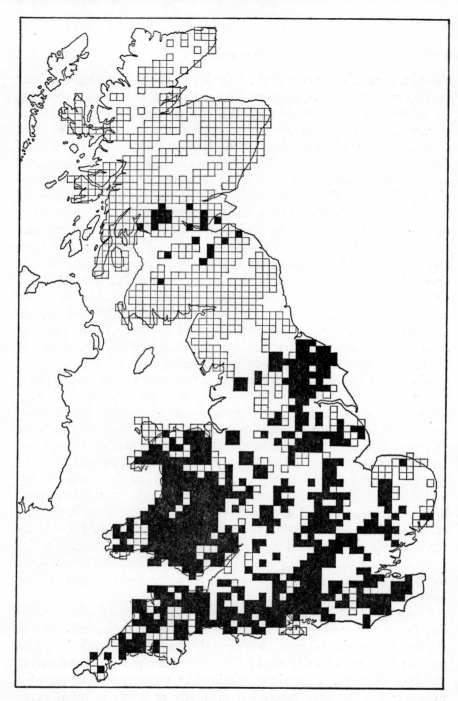

Distribution of grey squirrels (above) and red squirrels (opposite) in Forestry Commission land in 1974. The white 10km squares indicate Forestry Commission land, the black 10km squares indicate the presence of squirrels. Most Forestry Commission hardwoods are relatively young

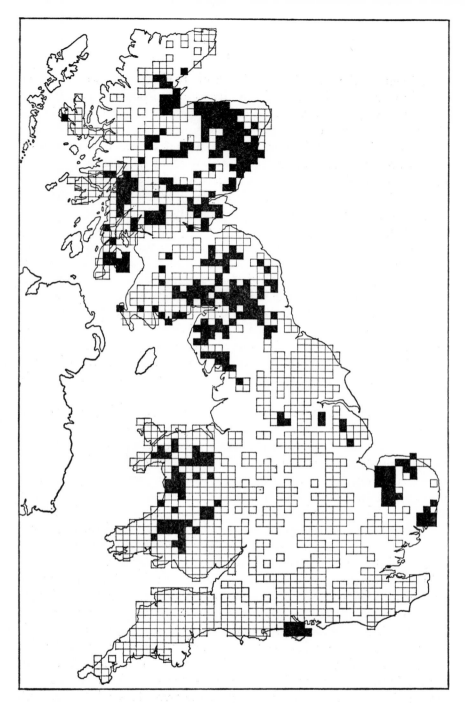

and therefore susceptible to damage. Large coniferous forests, such as in Wales, East Anglia and Scotland, provide refuge for red squirrels. By permission of the Forestry Commission.

the advent of the grey it occupied both habitats and has now been forced to retreat to its original one, where it too can be a pest. But no amount of propaganda will teach a nation reared on Squirrel Nutkin and Timmy Tiptoes not to love these round-nosed animals.

The period between the wars has often been described as disappointing in terms of progress towards the conservation of wildlife in Britain. In 1921 a remarkable speech in Manchester by T. A. Coward, perhaps the first full-time nature journalist, fell on deaf ears; in it he anticipated most of the reasons for conservation now generally accepted. But the necessary techniques for appraising distribution and numbers scientifically were being worked out, nowhere more industriously than at Oxford where the Bureau of Animal Population under Charles Elton and the Edward Grey Institute of Field Ornithology were the professional nuclei. The second was founded, like the amateur research body, the British Trust for Ornithology (1932), largely through the energies of Bernard Tucker and E. M. Nicholson, later to be Director-General of the Nature Conservancy. Far away in East Anglia, fathered by Dr S. H. Long, the formation in 1926 of the Norfolk Naturalists' Trust, to acquire and lease important nature reserves, seemed a lonely concept.

The war, which saw many people spending hours of unexpected inactivity in remote rural areas, was the catalyst that set in train an explosion of popular interest, spearheaded by ornithology and, in particular, by James Fisher's *Watching Birds*, the publication of which could not have been more timely. The presence of an eminent biologist, Julian Huxley, on the radio 'Brains Trust', was another favourable factor. There developed a hunger for books, for photographs, for field studies— the (now) Field Studies Council was set up in 1944—and for new clubs to channel the tide of enthusiasts. Radio and soon television enormously magnified the public interest in natural history programmes.

In the 1950s the county trust movement suddenly gained momentum until in 1965 the whole of Britain was covered by its branches under the auspices of the Society for the Promotion of Nature Reserves. In 1958 the Council for Nature was set up under royal patronage as an umbrella body for the whole voluntary conservation movement; one of its first moves was to found the Conservation Corps—now the independent British Trust for Conservation Volunteers—to undertake active management tasks on reserves. Membership of the two National Trusts, both with strong conservation interests, and of the Royal Society for the

Protection of Birds (1889) began a steep climb, the National Trust reaching its half million in 1975.

In 1949 the Nature Conservancy (now Nature Conservancy Council) was set up for the whole of Britain (there is a separate body in Northern Ireland) and now controls some quarter million acres of national nature reserves (there are 125,000 acres in voluntary hands). In 1954 a new Bird Protection Act was the first of a series of conservation measures, the latest being the Wild Plants and Wild Creatures Act of 1975. But legislation will only work if there is a vigorous public opinion behind it. To promote this is one of the tasks of the World Wildlife Fund, whose British section, set up in 1961, was the first of all. Thus amplified, the voice of the wildlife lobby is no longer still and small; the best loved flora and fauna in the world has weathered major crises and will no doubt meet others, but it now has effective champions.

CHAPTER 11

THE AMENITY MOVEMENT

Christopher Hall

We are apt to forget that the greatest historical monument that we possess, the most essential thing which is England, is the Countryside, the Market Town, the Village, the Hedgerow Trees, the Lanes, the Copses, the Streams and the Farmsteads. To destroy these and leave a considerable number of archaeological specimens neatly docketed and securely fenced off from a wilderness of slag-heaps or rubbish tips might satisfy the unadulterated antiquarian; but the plain man would lose his greatest possession – the country setting.

Is there indeed anything which Science or Mechanism may create to compensate an Englishman for the loss of the Countryside?

Thus Patrick Abercrombie, then Professor of Civic Design at Liverpool University, in the clarion pamphlet *The Preservation of Rural England* which—capitalised initials and all—he published in 1926. It was in this pamphlet that he called for the formation of a 'strong Joint Committee with representatives from a wide range of societies' to preserve 'the most essential thing which is England'. A few months later, on 7

December at 33 Bloomsbury Square that strong Joint Committee was formed and was christened the Council for the Preservation of Rural England.

CPRE was by no means the first organisation established to preserve the countryside either nationally or locally. Why therefore did Patrick Abercrombie feel it was so necessary in 1926? And why did he succeed in gathering together so many powerful bodies and influential individuals beneath its banner so swiftly?

What distinguished the CPRE from all predecessor organisations was the generality of its concern, and what gave it impetus (and has sustained it since) was the generality of the threat to the countryside which emerged in the 1920s and in different guises, sometimes muted, sometimes controlled, has persisted ever since.

The first national countryside preservation body was the Commons Preservation Society (now the Commons, Open Spaces and Footpaths Preservation Society) founded by John Stuart Mill and friends in 1865 with the aim of saving the last remaining great commons from enclosure. Later its remit was extended to the preservation of public paths. In both capacities it was naturally concerned with the beauties of the landscape, but it was and remains a specialist body concerned primarily with the defence of the public right to enjoy the countryside rather than with the quality of the scene.

The National Trust (full title: the National Trust for Places of Historic Interest and Natural Beauty) dates back to 1895 and had enjoyed the unique right to hold property inalienably since an Act of Parliament in 1907. The Trust operated then as now by purchasing land for its protection. But in its early years the Trust frequently sought to save from desecration territory which it did not own and could not hope to buy. Its historian, Robin Fedden, has claimed that as late as the 1930s the Trust sought to 'maintain almost single-handed the struggle to protect the best of the countryside'—a claim which would certainly have been true in the 1920s. Nevertheless the Trust could only be truly effective by ownership; this was at once its forte and its weakness.

Abercrombie's special vision was that the countryside could no longer be defended by saving a common here or buying a stately home there. The threats had become general; all men of good will must sink their specialist concerns and band together.

Reading Abercrombie's initial appeal today, one's first impression is of the familiarity of the issues: urban sprawl, new roads, crude afforestation, the poor standards of design of new housing in the countryside, the spread of power lines. The point is that these factors emerged in a new strength in the 1920s and simultaneously. Moreover, Abercrombie saw that the post-war expansion of these things had occurred for the most part in a period of economic depression. The threats would intensify with the revival of trade. Not only did Abercrombie and his colleagues see the necessity for a generalised response. They saw that even the strongest grouping of informed opinion would ultimately fail unless new statutory mechanisms for defending the countryside were instituted.

The keynote of the CPRE's style was respectability. It is not unusual to find a voluntary organisation starting life with a more or less revolutionary programme and gradually, as it wins acceptance and influence, becoming recognisably part of the establishment. The extraordinary thing about CPRE is that it was born respectable. CPRE's first President was the Earl of Crawford and Balcarres—CPRE has always set much store by possession of a voice in the upper House; its first Vice-President was Guy (later Sir Guy) Dawber, an architect. These two with Abercrombie (first Honorary Secretary) comprised the founding triumvirate. Herbert (later Sir Herbert) Griffin was the Secretary and remained so until 1965. Continuity is another feature of CPRE.

In the foreword to CPRE's first annual report, Sir William Beach Thomas wrote of CPRE as a federation, which it was. Within a year it had attracted as constituent members 24 established organisations including (to name only some which are still officially part of CPRE) the Royal Institute of British Architects, the (now Royal) Town Planning Institute, the County Councils Association, the National Federation of Women's Institutes, the Royal Automobile Club, the Automobile Association, the Urban District Councils Association, the Central (now Country) Landowners' Association, and the Garden Cities and Town Planning (now Town and Country Planning) Association.

CPRE's early strategy was to work on the assumption that everyone who was anyone must share its objectives. Other early writers of CPRE forewords were J. C. Squire in 1928, Hugh Walpole in 1929 and Edmund Blunden in 1930. Neville Chamberlain, then Minister of Health and responsible for such town and country planning as existed, spoke at its inaugural meeting and endorsed the infant Council's aims. In 1929—after CPRE had memorialised the party leaders of the day—*Punch* published a cartoon which showed Baldwin, Ramsay MacDonald and Lloyd George skipping through the fields in harmony of purpose on at least one subject, the preservation of rural England.

In practice these august gestures of goodwill meant little and the conglomeration of influential bodies which composed the Council were less than fully united. Some of the real difficulties facing the Council emerged in its first major battle to secure universal rural planning. The Labour Government of 1929–31 introduced a bill which would have ensured that development anywhere in the countryside could be controlled. It was warmly welcomed by CPRE. But the bill was emasculated after the election of 1931 in a House which was probably more hostile to interference with market forces than any other this century. A discreet paragraph in CPRE's annual report suggests that the bill's fate was largely due to opposition by the land-owning interest in Parliament.

Meanwhile another initiative had run into the sand. In 1929, following representations from CPRE, the government had set up a committee under the chairmanship of Dr Christopher Addison MP 'to consider and report if it is desirable and feasible to establish one or more National Parks in Great Britain. . . .' The Addison Committee duly reported that national parks were necessary 'if the present generation is to escape the charge that in a short-sighted pursuit of its immediate ends it has squandered a noble heritage'. The report appeared immediately prior to the election of 1931 and the economic blizzard which precipitated it—no time for environmental frills and the cause seemed quickly forgotten.

But as the 1930s progressed—fulfilling environmentally as well as in every other way Auden's epitaph upon 'a low dishonest decade'— CPRE, beavering in committees and among the well-heeled preservationists of the shires, did have some successes to chalk up. Ribbon development—'riband development' as the early CPRE reports quaintly term it—had always been a major CPRE target and in 1935 their efforts were crowned by the passage to the statute book of the Restriction of Ribbon Development Act which made it unlawful within 220ft of the middle of every classified highway 'to construct, form or lay out any means of access or to erect or make any building' without consent. Otherwise the 1930s remained a permissive decade so far as planning was concerned. The annual reports of CPRE are full of tales of representations to electricity undertakings and water authorities and the builders of roads. There was not much that CPRE could do to make its point stick on any of these things: the idea that the community, however indirectly, should settle the routes of roads and overhead power lines remained a distant ideal.

One notable CPRE success from these years deserves record. The Forestry Commission had been established in 1919 to build up the nation's strategic reserve of timber and had quickly won itself the reputation it still enjoys as an obliterator of fine landscapes. In the mid-1930s the Commission turned its eyes upon the Lake District and here it was checked. CPRE working closely with the local society, the Friends of the Lake District, entered upon prolonged negotiations with the Commission. At the same time the Rev H. H. Symonds, then perhaps the most trenchant propagandist of the amenity movement, smothered the Commission in a salutary gale of invective. In the end an agreement to prevent afforestation of the central Lakeland fells was secured.

Lord Crawford, in his presidential address to the CPRE's annual general meeting of 1936, spelled the moral: 'If we apply the generally accepted rules of town and country planning to afforestation we shall afforest in a manner which is useful to the community and which avoids any unnecessary disfigurement or obscuration.' Vain hopes; 40 years on and CPRE is still trying to bring afforestation within the ambit of planning, and the forestry industry still maintains its position of anomalous and abused privilege.

On paper one of the most hopeful signs of progress in the amenity movement was the growth of CPRE county branches during its early years, for these gave the individual an opportunity to join in and to seek to influence problems at a local level. The 1936 annual report lists 26 county branches or committees. For the most part these branches were deeply enmeshed in the local county establishments. Landed peers presided at their AGMs. When a new branch was formed it was usually the Lord Lieutenant who took the chair. Such was the CPRE of the mid-1930s and, some would say, of today: securely based in the landed gentry and the upper middle-classes, its representatives padding persuasively down the corridors of power, making a representation here, dropping a note of regret there; listening 'with attention' to the Minister; making some visible progress, but scarcely engendering an order of excitement or enthusiasm commensurate with the problems which had called it into being.

Upon this well ordered, English scene there burst in the 1930s a new wave of environmental concern—the open air movement of the towns or the 'hikers' as its most visible elements were known to the press. In the popular newspapers of the 1930s the hikers occupied the same place as 'drugs and teenagers' in the journalism of the 1960s. One Roman Catholic priest spoke of hiking's 'grave moral dangers'. When challenged by the movement's spokesmen he hurriedly explained that he had not meant hikers belonging to bona fide organisations. Not that hiking was seen as uniformly bad. There were many ready to recognise its healthful qualities. CPRE at first had little contact with this *nouvelle vague*, whose infusion was ultimately to strengthen its aims so greatly. CPRE's links were with the well established Commons Open Spaces and Footpaths Preservation Society (Secretary: Sir Lawrence Chubb).

Protection of public paths dated back at least to the 1820s and had been further nourished by the growth of rambling among the artisans' self-improvement societies of the north, the early south-eastern rambling clubs of the 1880s and the first significant federation of such clubs in London in 1906. Walking—always a literary pastime—had been passed down to the less bohemian middle classes in the guest houses of the Co-operative Holidays Association and Holiday Fellowship (both formed in Edwardian years).

In the late twenties and early thirties this relatively esoteric pastime suddenly became a mass pleasure. Its growth can be traced in the pages of *The Hiker and Camper*, a magazine started in 1931. Associate Editor of the new magazine and contributing frequently was Commander J. M. Kenworthy RN, a maverick Labour MP. The flavour of the magazine can be judged from this poem which appeared without attribution in the first issue:

> Oh! Youth and maid, come with me,
> Be happy, jolly, healthy, free;
> For o'er the Downs we will walk,
> And on some pleasant subjects talk;
> View nature's work and countryside,
> Hedge-rows and flowers, vistas wide
> Of waving meadows, changing skies,
> Beauty unfolding to the eyes;
> Down in the dale, hear murm'ring rill,
> Tread sun-lit wood, then climb the hill
> And take a glimpse of shore and sea –
> Oh! Youth and maiden come with me.

Kenworthy seems to have wanted the whole 'youth movement' or 'open-air movement' (both phrases appear and almost interchangeably) to have more precisely defined aims than these romantic blatherings. At times there was more than a touch of Nazi 'strength through joy' in his ideas, as for instance when he and the magazine organised a great hikers' and campers' rally at Portsmouth to coincide with Navy Week.

From Germany Britain had already borrowed the youth hostel idea. The Youth Hostel Association's first six hostels opened for Easter 1931 and within two years there were 150 of them, catering for an active membership of some 20,000, three-quarters of whom were under 25. Its first President was Professor G. M. Trevelyan OM. The Camping Club had shot from a membership of 4,000 in 1930 to 5,500 a year later. Federations of rambling clubs (on the model of the existing one in the south-east), in formation around the country, grew into a loose National Council in 1931, which in 1935 became the Ramblers' Association.

The power potential of this new movement was considerable, though scarcely realised by its promoters and leaders. The commercial world understood better.

> 'I'm happy when I'm hiking,
> Pack upon my back'

ran the lyric of a song which in 1930 made the equivalent of the Top Twenty. Mass advertisers like Horlicks and Branston Pickles bought space in *The Hiker and Camper*. The same magazine in one of its first issues carried an advertisement by a speculative builder: 'Live at Banstead: the starting point of your rambles. Prices from £850—freehold including garage.' The picture alongside showed Banstead poised at the apex of railway lines radiating southwards into the Surrey and Sussex countryside.

Politicians were interested too. Most of the glory of the famous mass trespass on Kinder Scout in the Peak District in 1932 is now given to the Ramblers' Association and there are members of the Association who are not averse to accepting the credit. In fact the Ramblers' Association had not even been formed in 1932 and the mass trespass was not organised or even approved by the Manchester and Sheffield Ramblers' Federations. It was organised by the British Workers' Sports Federation, a Communist Party front organisation. The mass trespass was nevertheless the inevitable outcome of years of hostility between the walkers and the landowners on the Derbyshire moors. A situation which might have been controlled prior to World War I was necessarily explosive as the number of hikers increased. As Cyril Joad—a great champion of the ramblers—remarked at the Sheffield and Manchester Ramblers' annual access demonstration the following year: 'Rambling has replaced beer as the shortest cut out of Manchester.'

The savage results of the mass trespass did not deflect the Ramblers from the path of constitutional reform. Six young men were jailed: one of them, accused of grievous bodily harm against a keeper, for six months, others for shorter periods. The official ramblers, though they had themselves held aloof from the trespass, were deeply shocked. The Manchester Federation petitioned the Home Secretary to intervene but the 'Liberal' Sir Herbert Samuel could not find grounds for so doing.

This incident, peripheral as it was to the mainstream of the campaign for access to mountains and moorlands, reinforced the natural prejudice of the walkers against the landowners. The Manchester Ramblers spoke of a 'reactionary Government'. An element of social and political conflict had come to the amenity movement and must have caused unease among people like Herbert Griffin and Sir Lawrence Chubb. Indeed, their efforts to bring the demands of the urban amenity movement within the spectrum of their own activities were less than wholly successful. To do so was not easy for plainly there was a conflict of interest between the CPRE (with its close affiliations with the landowners) and the Ramblers. In 1939 an anonymous writer in the Manchester Federation of Rambling Clubs' handbook, probably Edwin Royce, the ablest Ramblers' leader in this period, wrote:

> At the Chester conference of the CPRE last October, a south country colonel suggested that rights of way should not necessarily be inviolable when they conflicted with efficient agriculture. Grand word 'efficient' and naturally it would be the colonel wallahs and their friends who would decide what was efficient. They are still with us, the old gang, who enclosed commons and snaffled footpaths, waiting, waiting and discussing the possibilities, against the time when the restrictive methods of the new bandits can be applied in this country.

Besides access to mountains and the protection of rights of way the ramblers and their associates were very much concerned with one early campaign of the CPRE—the pressure for national parks. In November 1935 George Mitchell, Secretary of the newborn Ramblers' Association and of the Joint Committee of Open-air Organisations, convened a conference in London at which the Standing Committee on National Parks was set up. The resolution to this effect was moved by Patrick Aber-crombie and the new body thus brought together all wings of the amenity movement.

Disunity persisted on the problem of public access to the wilder countryside. An 'access to mountains' bill had been introduced as long ago as 1884 and had twice got as far as a second reading. In 1938 Mr Arthur Creech-Jones MP tried again, and got his private member's bill as far as an unopposed second reading. It was a simple bill and would have ended the civil tort of trespass on all land designated. But it now became clear that the landowners were not going to have it and their spokesmen were a great deal more numerous and influential in the Commons of 1938 than today.

Sir Lawrence Chubb tried to mediate. He worked out a compromise which would in theory have given the right of access to all uncultivated land, but the landowner would be enabled to appeal to the minister of agriculture for an order to restrict access or subject it to conditions. It would have been an offence to ignore such restrictions or conditions, thus creating a criminal offence of trespass for the first time ever. After further negotiations the bill emerged as a cumbersome piece of mach-inery for securing access by piecemeal designations. The offences it created made it anathema to the rambling organisations, among whom Sir Lawrence was now widely regarded as a traitor to the cause.

The war now looming and its aftermath were to change the whole planning scene. They served to place in power politicians personally sympathetic to the aims of the amenity movement and to create in Whitehall and Westminster a mood favourable to the interventionist policies it advocated. The groundwork was laid during the war years. The epoch-marking reports of the Barlow Commission (location of industry), and the Scott Committee (rural land utilisation) were clearly influenced by the amenity societies which presented detailed evidence to them. The Standing Committee on National Parks, first with Symonds and then John Dower as its drafting secretary, had produced a vital pamphlet, *The Case for National Parks*, in 1938 and Dower himself wrote the seminal Government-sponsored report of 1945 which proved ultimately to be the basis for the national parks legislation of 1949.

The pivotal role in this period of the amenity movement belongs to the Ramblers' Association. Politically and socially their leaders were in tune both with the spirit of the times and the leading figures in the 1945 Labour Government. Tom Stephenson, who had previously worked in

Transport House and on the *Daily Herald*, did not become Secretary of the RA until 1948, but he had coined the idea of the Pennine Way (borrowed in fact from the American Appalachian Trail) in 1935 and had played a prominent part in the association formed to promote it. In 1945 he was press officer at the Ministry of Town and Country Planning when, in December 1945, the Minister, Mr Lewis Silkin, received a deputation from the RA. Stephenson drafted the ensuing press release which declared the Minister's intention of legislating for national parks, access to mountains and long-distance paths. A few months later Hugh Dalton, then Chancellor of the Exchequer, established a National Land Fund of £50 million as 'a nest egg, set aside, which could be used to finance some of the operations necessary in order to give to the public permanent access to the national parks'. In 1947 the Hobhouse Committee reported, clothing the national park and long-distance path ideas in more detail. Its footpath sub-committee called for a complete national survey of all public paths.

The RA now mounted and led the campaign to persuade the government to find time for the legislation. Monster meetings—1,600 in Kingsway Hall, London, to hear John Cripps (the Editor of *The Countryman*), the Rt Hon James Chuter Ede (then Home Secretary and a keen rambler), Viscount Samuel and Geoffrey Winthrop Young; and 1,500 at Birmingham to hear Silkin, Joad and Francis Ritchie—were its main feature.

A landmark of the campaign was the walk along part of the proposed Pennine Way which Tom Stephenson led at Whitsuntide 1948. His MP companions included Hugh Dalton (by then President of the RA), Barbara Castle, Arthur Blenkinsop, George Chetwynd, Geoffrey de Freitas and Fred Willey.

The campaign succeeded in that it produced the monumental National Parks and Access to the Countryside Act of 1949. It failed in that the Act fell short of its promoters' hopes. The Act provided less than adequate representation of the national interest in national park authorities and left a loophole whereby multi-county national parks were able to escape without the independent planning boards Parliament had envisaged for them. In the event only two such boards—for the Peaks and the Lakes—were established. Most disappointing of all to the ramblers were the access provisions. The Hobhouse Committee had recommended a survey of uncultivated land, publication of a statutory map showing uncultivated land open to public access. Instead the Act merely enabled local authorities to make access agreements and this option was not taken up seriously outside the Peak District where the council-landowner agreements proved an acceptable solution to the edgy disputes of the 1930s.

On the other hand, so far as rights of way were concerned, by providing for statutory mapping and consequent safeguards, the Act gave the walkers pretty well all they wanted. The subsequent implementation of the Act by the local authorities, some of which have still not completed their definitive maps more than a quarter of a century after the legislation, has been less than satisfactory.

The other vital Act of the immediate post-war years for the amenity movement was the 1947 Planning Act. This wrote into the statute book the essential definition of change of use which still prevails and for which the permission of the local planning authority is required. This control, in combination with the requirement to produce development plans, has made possible all the protective zoning of land which has been the bread and butter of the amenity societies, national and local, ever since. The Scott report had recommended that any developer should bear the onus of proof that it was in the public interest to change the use of existing rural land. The 1947 Act did not, in so many words, provide for this. But that was the spirit of the legislation.

Yet oddly the Act seems not to have been greeted with any great enthusiasm by the amenity movement. The CPRE in its relevant annual report clearly regarded the problem of winning land back from the Services as the most important issue of the year. More and typically perceptive was the brief comment by Francis Ritchie, later a National Parks Commissioner, writing in *Countrygoer*: 'It is reasonable to hope that this [Act] will prove to be a turning point in the so-far ineffectual struggle for rural preservation.'

It is no accident that we are now more than halfway through this chapter but barely at the mid-point of the 50 years under review. For around 1950, with the end of the spate of post-war legislation planning, comes a natural break. Hitherto the story has been one of struggle: the struggle to secure the statutory framework which the pioneers—notably Abercrombie, Dower and Stephenson—saw to be essential. The last 25 years have been largely devoted to the more mundane business of getting the best possible results from that legislation. Indeed it was not until the 1960s that there began to emerge new and exciting elements in the amenity scene.

In the 1950s both CPRE and the RA seemed sunk in peace, though not lethargy. There were battles to secure the designation of national parks, often against stern local authority opposition and the failure to secure adequate administration for them. CPRE was successful in persuading the government to take a strong line in favour of green belts. The RA was involved in the detailed work of ensuring that the statutory footpath maps were as comprehensive as possible and since the mid-1960s they have been engaged in a running battle with the farmers' and landowners' organisations and a few local authorities who wish to 'rationalise' the path network into a tiny shadow of itself.

The entire amenity movement was engaged in the vain efforts to prevent Manchester's depredations of Ullswater and the flooding of Cow Green in upper Teesdale in the 1960s. Afforestation remained a problem which the movement sought in vain to bring under adequate control. And, despite continual pressure, farm buildings of ever-increasing ugliness continued to escape development control. The makers of the planning framework in the 1940s had assumed that farming equals conservation, an equation which the agricultural revolution rendered out of date, until in 1975, despite hostility from its constituent members the NFU and CLA, CPRE felt compelled to press for a degree of control over the destruction of hedges and the ploughing of moors, downs and heaths.

The Ramblers, supported by other societies, played a leading role in the campaign to secure independent planning boards for all national parks, a reform for which the Local Government Act 1972 appeared to provide an opportunity. However the Countryside Commission, which had steadfastly supported such a change, preferred not to tangle with the county councils and the Department of the Environment was only too glad to fall in with their views.

From the late 1950s onwards the gradual extension of the motorway network provides a recurring theme in the reports of all the amenity societies, sometimes breaking out in *causes célèbres* such as the routing of the M40 over the Chilterns and the M4 over the Berkshire Downs. But, significantly, the amenity movement mounted no fundamental challenge to the roads programme until the mid-1970s.

The fact is that the amenity societies had ceased to think much about first principles. Having secured the most sophisticated land-use planning system in the world they were understandably content to limit their efforts to making the system work. Moreover, their leaders were ageing.

Sir Herbert Griffin and Tom Stephenson were both in their seventies when they ultimately relinquished their posts as secretaries of CPRE and the RA in 1965 and 1968 respectively.

The new countryside legislation of the 1960s owed little to the amenity societies (the tree preservation and conservation area measures promoted by the Civic Trust apart). Whereas the great legislation of the 1940s bore the visible imprint of Abercrombie, Dower and Stephenson, the Countryside Act 1968 did not; nor did the first basic change in planning since 1947—the introduction of structure to replace development plans in 1968.

But there were new stirrings. The Civic Trust, founded in 1957, itself encouraged and reflected the growth in local civic societies. Though, as their generic name implies, not concerned with the countryside, these societies were important because they tended to recruit members and leaders from among the younger professional middle-classes to whom the CPRE had not much appealed.

There was a general quickening in environmental concern towards the end of the 1960s. The three *Countryside in 1970* conferences— attended by all the good and great with an interest in the environment —marked this interest, though it is hard in retrospect to see what they positively achieved. The co-ordinating Committee for Environmental Conservation which flowed directly from the conferences has made little impact.

The real impact of recent years has come from a new type of environmental concern, which takes the whole planet and the question of whether a sustainable life-style can be maintained upon it, for its remit. Organisations like the Conservation Society (1966) and Friends of the Earth (1971) reflect this new concern and, in contrast to the older environmentalist groups, may be classed as 'anti-growth'. At the extreme this takes the form of believing that only a society organised in agrarian communes can ultimately survive. The 'anti-growth' societies have not been directly concerned with the countryside, but have often worked alongside bodies such as the Ramblers and CPRE on particular issues, such as resisting copper mining in Snowdonia and in opposing road schemes.

I do not foresee the established amenity movement declaring an overtly anti-growth platform in the reckonable future. Too many of the movement's members would accept Tony Crosland's view that growth is essential to finance the improvement of most people's environment.

If you would like to buy further copies
of THE COUNTRYMAN'S BRITAIN, they are
available at £5.25. We will make no
charge for packing and postage.

ORDER FORM

The Countryman, 23-27 Tudor Street, LONDON
EC4Y OHR.

Please supply .... copies of THE
COUNTRYMAN'S BRITAIN at £5.25 ($8.50)
per copy. I understand there is no
charge for postage and packing. I enclose
remittance for ....

NAME : ....

ADDRESS : ....

....

....

(In block capitals please)

But the influence of the anti-growth school is considerable. CPRE today for instance is ready to challenge the growth assumptions underlying the roads programme in a way that would have been unthinkable four or five years ago. At the same time it is sceptical of the grandiose growth strategies of the regional planners. No doubt the true anti-growth man, while welcoming such *ad hoc* support, must find it odd and muddled that this support is not accompanied by conversion to his philosophy. But the *ad hoc* compromisers of the amenity movement are probably closer to the practicalities of the situation and will in the end push the government of the day further towards modest and sensible policies in line with the true capacities of the nation's resources, than those who insist on the pure milk of the anti-growth doctrine. Such, at any rate, is my hope.

CHAPTER 12

ECONOMIC GROWTH

Tony Aldous

THE IMPACT of economic growth on the countryside in the half century
from 1927 has been immense and varied. In that period Britain has become in all sorts of ways a more urban, or *urbanised*, country. Big cities
have grown, not always in population, but invariably in their acreages;
small and medium-sized towns have sprouted space-consuming suburbs;
and many villages have grown to look like small towns. At the same time
the needs of these urban populations have imposed all manner of more-
or-less alien artefacts even on countryside which escaped the direct
spread of the towns: bigger and bigger reservoirs to feed the thirsty
towns and their industry; wider and faster roads to link them together;
more and larger-scale quarrying, gravel and china clay extraction, and
open-cast coal mining; ever-bigger power stations and power lines to
link them; the essentially urban rush and frenzy of North Sea oil and gas
exploitation—all these have made a prodigious physical and visual impact on Britain's countryside.

But, psychologically and socially, the effects go deeper and further.
Urban assumptions and instincts have permeated much of our countryside: the rural economy depends more and more on urban props. Be-

tween the 1931 and 1971 censuses, Britain's rural population rose from 9·5 to 12 million. More significantly the proportion of the total population living in rural areas rose from around 21 to well over 23 per cent. But the number of full-time agricultural workers continued to drop: in 1927, 894,000; in 1931, 829,000; in 1961, 449,000; and in 1974 306,000. The inference to be drawn from these figures is clear: the proportion of countrymen actually earning their living on the land has shrunk, is shrinking and will very likely continue to shrink.

The new countrymen and countrywomen who account for the growth in numbers are to a very large extent urban in origin—commuters, retired people, escapers from the rat-race who find a way of earning a living in countryside instead of town. But they almost all have one thing in common: most or all of their income comes from the town. And this economic dependence tells. Be they ever so enthusiastic CPRE members in the home counties or journalists-turned-subsistence-farmers in wild West Wales, their instincts and some of their money or earning power are town-oriented, and this constitutes a dillution of 'countryness'. They are an unwitting urban fifth column undermining rural independence.

This 'economic dilution' argument is perhaps open to challenge, at any rate as to degree. What is scarcely open to question is the impact of physical change brought about by economic growth. Here scale is all-important. The 50 years from 1927 were pre-eminently years in which urban man and his institutions assumed that Bigger was Better and Big was Best—an assumption inimical to conservation of rural landscape and rural society. In a sense, the tragedy of the countryside in that half-century has been that Small ceased, economically speaking, to be Beautiful. Economy of scale was the economic doctrine which impelled so many and diverse physical changes in our rural areas.

The growth of cities and towns themselves: Ministry of Agriculture statistics show that in recent years 'development' of various kinds has tended to take more and more productive agricultural land: 33,000 acres a year on average during the quinquennium 1961–66, more than 49,000 a year from 1966–71, and nearly 70,000 acres a year from 1968–73. But contrary to popular assumption, this is not an unprecedented peak. During the great urban and suburban expansions of the 1930s, the 'take' of farmland for urban uses ran at very much the same level as in 1968–73. Until this last quinquennium we were losing considerably less farmland to urban uses than during the 1930s peak.

In other ways these crude 'loss of productive land' figures may mislead the casual reader. Dr Robin Best of Wye College has demonstrated that loss of agricultural acres does not always coincide with population gain. In the 1960s and early '70s, Durham and Lancashire lost more agricultural land than most other areas but also suffered absolute losses of population. Some possible reasons for this are evident on the ground. Modern industrial complexes like the ICI chemical works on Teesside take large areas of land but provide relatively few jobs: they are capital intensive and highly automated. Dr Best argues that industry in the 1960s and '70s is (partly because of tighter planning control) much less prodigal of rural acres. But it is also larger scale; and here we can usefully make another important distinction. Just as 'loss of productive land' and 'loss of countryside' are not the same thing, so also the acreage of the urban 'take' is not at all the same thing as its impact. A chemical works by the sea may consume 100 acres, but if it is visible from a long stretch of coast and a wide area of surrounding hills, its impact is out of all proportion to its area. On the other hand, if it is sited in a large disused quarry and screened by planting, both its impact and its qualitative land take could be minimal.

Nor does this urban impact concern only landscape. The effect on countryside and farming of having a town and townsmen as neighbours shows itself most devastatingly on the urban (or rather suburban) fringes of big conurbations. Even where Green Belt policies halt the sprawl, the city seems to breathe invisible urban fumes into the adjacent farmland—fumes poisoned with alien urban values and assumptions. The experimental project started in 1975 by the Countryside Commission in a 210 sq km area on the borders of London and Hertfordshire demonstrates this. Alan Hall, the project officer, took me to, among other places, a stretch of 'fringe' countryside near Edgware gripped for years by a continuous state of cold (and sometimes hot) war between town and country. At the backs of streets of 1950s council housing, a thin screen of scrub-cum-spinney lay knee-deep in rubbish ranging from plastic bags and cola cans to mattresses, broken furniture and even half a car. Yet the adjacent gardens were in many cases the epitome of cultivated neatness.

Of the relations between these townsmen and their farmer neighbours, Alan Hall says: 'It's not so much hostility as sheer incomprehension that divides them.' The incomprehension is not confined to council tenants— stockbrokers have been known to let their dogs play in fields of young crops on the apparent assumption that this is just so much extra unmown parkland. On the other side of the fence, a psychological barrier seems to prevent most farmers (admittedly hard-pressed) from taking a positive attitude towards urban recreational needs. Alan Hall's project, sponsored jointly for three years by the Countryside Commission and three local authorities, seeks, by a mixture of physical patching and improving and psychological bridge-building, to improve the urban fringe both in appearance and in neighbour relations.

At Edgwarebury other symptoms of the urban-fringe malaise could be seen in the landscape. Farmers in such areas, tired of coping with gates left open, hedges and fences forced down, plastic bags for cows to swallow and uncontrolled dogs, have generally long ago turned to arable farming. But Hall reckons that in the urban-fringe situation they instinctively pursue a landscape-denuding policy. They pull out hedges not just because large fields are more economic, but because they sense that these are less attractive to potentially destructive urban intruders. He pointed out to me one line of trees that marked a now non-existent hedge. Half the trees were stag-headed. Left to itself, in 20 years this little piece of edge-of-town landscape could be devoid of vertical feature. The area's productivity increased, no doubt, but to most eyes greatly diminished in appearance.

Greater agricultural productivity does however demand bigger fields for the efficient use of bigger and better machines. John Weller cites the graphic but not so untypical example of 'one progressive farmer, Mr J. J. Rainthorpe, with 2,300 acres near Lincoln, who has cleared 48 miles of boundary hedge and tiled and filled $8\frac{1}{4}$ miles of open ditch. The original eight farms, having 135 fields with an average of 15 acres each, have been amalgamated into one farm with only 33 fields averaging 60 acres each.' But for the demands of three post-war decades of economic growth, that degree of 'Progress' would scarcely have been demanded of him.

But the main invasion of the countryside by townsmen has not been over the back fences of suburban estates, but by the great, threatening mobile columns of the open-air leisure explosion. Here we will consider not recreational pressure itself but the spate of road-building which both made it possible and further stimulated it. The actual acreage taken by road building is not inconsiderable—the CPRE estimate it as running at some 3,100 acres each year, and Britain's first much vaunted 1,000 miles of motorway must alone have taken something over 40,000 acres. But again land take is not a true measure of impact. Severance and intrusion go far beyond acreage. Thus the best efforts of the Department of the Environment's landscape architects and its advisory committee on choice of routes may still leave a tranquil and relatively unspoiled landscape transformed into something neither unspoiled nor ever again completely tranquil. Trees may grow a screen against the visual intrusion of a constantly moving stream of vehicles; earth-moving machinery may pile up skilfully moulded banks that contain most of the noise. But at the end of that walk through the woods or that drive along a meandering country lane, what have you? A great, out-of-scale artefact filled with restlessness and noise in totally unrural proportions and quantities. It is one of those ironies of democratic institutions that Barbara Castle, sometime Minister of Transport, can no longer bear to take one of her favourite Chilterns walks because her own road engineers later sliced the M40 through it in a cutting.

Much has been written in recent years about severance of urban communities by motorways; but the effect on rural communities (though the numbers of people affected may to urban-eyed road engineers seem insignificant) can be equally damaging. The village of Rownhams in Hampshire was a case in point. Villagers had long known that the M27 south coast motorway would pass close by, but did not discover until too late that it would sever one of the main streets, cutting off a substantial group of houses from the main body of the village. The villagers tried to move the road half a mile north. Too expensive, said the Ministry. They asked for a skew bridge to preserve a direct (rather than circuitous) link between the two parts of the village; again too expensive. After a public inquiry, the inspector and the Minister accepted the cost argument at the price of considerable inconvenience to local people. But this was not the end of the affair. By a later and separate procedure villagers found themselves faced with a proposal to site a motorway service area on the very edge of the village. This would include petrol pumps, repair facilities, restaurants and snack bars and all the other impedimenta of such places.

Rownhams saw the writing on the wall: holiday traffic in summer, docks traffic all the year round; 24-hours-a-day revving of engines, slamming of doors and glare from headlights and 24ft high lighting masts all making life in the eastern end of the village intolerable. They fought the service area issue too, but lost. Basically, it seems, a peaceful life for these few hundred Hampshire villagers weighed light in the public inquiry scales against road planners' arguments that this was the optimum position for a service area and that it would be easier to recruit staff for the restaurants and other facilities in a village location than in the secluded alternative site proposed by the residents. In January 1976 the road opened and Mr Jack Parker, who as chairman of the residents association and a rural councillor had played a prominent part in fighting it, reported that some of his fellow villagers nearer the road were 'undergoing torture' from traffic noise and visual intrusion. Many of them, he pointed out, were people who had come to live in this quiet Hampshire village specifically to enjoy its rustic tranquility. The foundations of the service area had been laid, he said, promising that when traffic justifies and economic conditions allow, Rownhams will have the privilege of playing unwilling host to thousands of passing motorists en route for the New Forest, Dorset and Devon—some of them no doubt in search of the very qualities of rustic repose that they will unwittingly ruin here in Hampshire.

The Rownhams experience represents what may be called the *Catch 22* of rural-urban conflict of interest: however persuasively you argue against damaging development in the countryside, the Big Battalions are almost always battalions of townsmen; the arguments are weighed either on the basis of crude economic gain or (more recently) by cost benefit calculations; but in either case, the accounting is done in townsmen's currency. When road engineers throw into the scale tens of thousands of road travellers' hours lost or gained, a pleasant and a tranquil life for 600 Hampshire villagers appears insignificant. When provision of a fast trunk road through the Lake District was the price of bringing a multi-million pound motor works to the ailing towns of west Cumberland, the most persuasive arguments of the Countryside Commission and the amenity lobby for not spoiling the scale and peace of the National Park failed to dislodge highly destructive plans for 'improving' the A66.

Motorways and trunk roads are really only the more noticeable features of a much more widespread process: the rising tide of motor traffic in the countryside and the highway engineer's attempt to channel and facilitate its flow by 'irrigation' techniques—by widening and straightening the 'streams' and 'culverts'. This drainage metaphor applied to roads and traffic is not as fanciful as it might seem. The instinct of both drainage and highway engineers is: 'If something blocks or impedes the flow, get rid of it.' That may be an acceptable policy with water, but its effect if applied to roads and traffic is often ruinous.

The results of this 'county surveyor's itch' to widen and straighten can be seen on the B2060 road through the Alkham valley in East Kent. This is a wandering country road running between the A2 and the A260 about three miles behind and parallel to the coast between Dover and Folkestone. Its primary purpose is to serve a series of village and farming communities in what is still a remarkably unspoiled stretch of the Kentish hinterland. But the road offers, or seems to offer, a quick short cut for car and lorry drivers wanting to get from the A2 to the A20 or vice versa. The response of Kent county highways engineers has been to 'improve' the road—to cater for this extraneous traffic as well as the increasing volumes of genuinely local traffic having its origin or destination in the valley. The southern end has been widened and straightened: it invites the motorist to go at 50mph rather than 35mph. It is a strip of town in the countryside. The northern end meanders; it has hedges, and its grass verges are not excessively tidy. The occasional building juts out perversely into or over the road; generally speaking it follows the natural contour and shape of the valley. It still looks and feels like countryside.

At least three reasons offer themselves for curbing the highwaymen's tidying and 'improving' tactics. The first is visual: straight, wide roads offend our sense of the informality of the countryside. To what extent this objection is romantic or subjective, peculiar to a generation used to a small-scale 'old-fashioned' pattern of fields and lanes, is open to argument. But if we place great store by the refreshing qualities of the rural scene, clearly urban-style roads are a loss. The second objection also concerns amenity. The widening and straightening strategy eventually demands the removal of buildings in the wrong place from the road-improvers' point of view: the awkward kink or corner, the double bend at the entrance to a village. It is, however, a sad fact that what irks the speeding motorist often charms the eye of visitor and villager alike. The chances are high, in the nature of things, that the awkwardly placed building is also an old and interesting one. Yet if all else on the line of route is straightened, then conservationists may find themselves confronted with the topsy-turvy argument that the safety of the speeding motorist requires that he should not be hindered at that point!

The third objection goes somewhat deeper. It protests that village roads are for villagers and their visitors, not for container traffic or tourists in a hurry to make the 10.30 boat to Boulogne, and that highways policy and techniques ought to be directed to discouraging such through traffic, to keeping it on trunk roads and motorways. After all, experience of the longer term effect of such road improvements as by-passes generally shows that, on Day 1 after the bypass opening, you can hear a pin drop in the High Street. The relief is marvellous. Three years later the traffic has started creeping back again; five years after, traffic flows are as heavy as they ever were. To some extent this reflects growth in car ownership and use in the local population. But it also confirms a sort of Parkinsonian Rule of the Road; traffic increases to fill the space available. Our hope must be that a new breed of county surveyor will come into power, who will itch, not to widen country roads like the B2060 where they turn off from the trunk road, but to narrow them—to build in pinch points and road layouts which discourage superfluous traffic. The prudent drainage engineer not only builds his great forty-foot drain to carry the main flow, but fits sluices to guard the countryside from inundation when the tide rises.

In passing, it should be noted that Britain's road builders do not always and only take rural acres for roads. When the M4 was extended westward round Reading, a short spur of motorway towards Maiden-head Thicket became redundant. Its ten acres of road surface were broken up and reinstated for agriculture, and sold (at a loss) back to farm-ing. This represents a small but commendable gesture in favour of rural rather than urban values; but it is so untypical that it serves chiefly to demonstrate how urban-oriented and urbanising in its effect Britain's road programme has been.

Landscaping and choice of routes have improved enormously in the past two or three decades, as the contrast between the early southern stretches of the M1 and recent stretches of motorway like the Gordano viaduct on the M5 and the M4 in Berkshire shows. But landscaping, however creative (as distinct from cosmetic), does not answer the initial hard question: ought a road to go here at all? Plans for a second trans-Pennine motorway through the northern part of the Peak District national park highlight the arguments. The conservationists, including the park authority, hold that a motorway, however well designed, is incompatible with preservation of this exceptionally beautiful country-side. The pro-motorway lobby retorts: 'What's the good of scenic beauty if no-one can see it?'

This argument is, of course, fallacious. Driving at 70mph is not the best way to appreciate even large-scale scenic beauty; and conversely you do not need a motorway in order to drive into a national park.

Moreover, wild countryside has qualities which to some extent depend on inaccessibility. We should not be accused of elitism for refusing to encourage our motorised urban masses to turn beauty spots into traffic jams. Recreational pressures on national parks vividly pose the conflict between quantitative urban and qualitative rural values. A count of urban number plates proves no more about quality than counting the cash in urban bank accounts.

Reservoirs have been another big expression of urban economic growth. As townsmen are better housed, they use more water; but domestic use is small as compared with the demands of industry. The 70,000 acres of land now under water for this purpose needs to grow by 2,000 acres every year, largely to satisfy the thirsty cities. From an amenity point of view, the result may not be bad. A dammed valley may suffer in time of drought from an ugly tide-mark, but in the so-called Somerset Lake District, for instance, fewer and fewer people remember or regret the old Chew Valley of farms and hedges and meandering river. They think instead of the present lake in its saucer of green fields, of picnics and fishing and the gentle lapping of lake water on the shore.

The same will almost certainly be true of the controversial Kielder reservoir in Northumberland, fought so strongly by local communities and conservationists. In terms of national interest, the sacrifices suffered did not seem to the minister or public opinion to begin to outweigh the gains to be had by building the reservoir. But 'national interest' generally means 'urban interest'. For the farmer I talked to in the to-be-flooded part of Kielder in 1974, it meant that what was left of his farm became unworkable; his chances of finding another he could afford out of compensation money were meagre; his house would be under the water and the community of which his family formed part would be severely disrupted if not destroyed.

To such countrymen, the arguments of the greatest good of the greatest number sound alien and out of touch with rural reality. They are abstractions that scarcely relate to the real world of earth and animals and stone walls, trees and hedges, wind and weather. Young architects might dream up splendid schemes for holiday cabins among the trees above the lake; my farmer knew that the slope never gets any sunlight after 1 pm! His experience of townsmen planning for a world they neither know nor understand is not new. In her book *The Valley*, Elizabeth Clarke tells of the coming of a reservoir to a remote rural valley in Radnorshire in the 1890s. She tells of Welsh farmers in their woven woollen coats, woollen breeches and polished black leggings and boots going to give evidence to a House of Commons select committee. One old farmer from the head of the valley seemed to speak for them all.

> Step by step the committee led him, through reassurances about his rights, to the agreement they sought, that he wanted no more. Had he any objection in itself, they asked, to Birmingham Corporation becoming owner of the property? 'No,' he said, 'I only wish for things to be as they are.'

Rural man presumably in the 1930s and '40s lost that hope or expectation. But he still faces townsmen who, like the 1892 Select Committee, think they know it all but make elementary mistakes such as confusing heather with stable litter. It makes little difference if they do understand. As Mrs Clarke points out, 'the moment industry's race for water began, our valley's destiny was inevitable'.

The extractive industries have also taken and still take their toll. The CPRE estimates that each year quarrying and aggregates extraction need 6,000 acres of countryside, without counting open-cast coal extraction. The way in which this industry has changed in the 50 years *The Countryman* has been publishing provides a specially graphic testimony to the impact of economic growth and new technology on the face of the countryside. In the 1920s quarries were still small-scale and local. They were as most of us still think of them: a hole in the hill the size of a small field, with a couple of lorries in it taking gravel for local road mending, or stone or slate for local building needs.

The reality is well exemplified at Cheddar—not the gorge, but the side of Cheddar the inhabitants are more conscious of than are visitors. Batts Coombe Quarry is a gash in the hillside 500yd wide and still growing, a series of giant steps on which lorries and dumper trucks look as insignificant as ants scuttling about their business. At Sandford Hill nearby, on the western end of the Mendips, the craggy, turfy top of pre-war years has gone. The hill is being quarried out like a hollow tooth. Here an existing planning permission would allow the quarry company to enlarge the width of the quarry entrance to 500 metres—wider than the world's tallest building is high. In 1947, the total take from all the quarries in the old county of Somerset, in 25 centuries of small quarrying, totalled no more than 50m tons. Twenty-five years later, in 1972, the cumulative total had doubled to more than 100 million tons. The quarry companies, in their own defence, say: 'This is what society demands when it asks for and expects new schools, new hospitals, new roads.' Modern quarrying does not, however, end with the physical and visual impact of extraction. The minerals have to be moved to where they are needed. Sometimes they go by rail—one firm in the eastern Mendips has built a new branch line and railhead. More often the route is by road, and for the first few miles of the journey unsuitable roads, as many residents of Cheddar are acutely aware, as a stream of noisy lorries clatter past their houses and round tight bends not meant to take them.

In some respects the picture has improved. In the 1920s, a firm like English China Clay would have bought land and done much as it wanted with it without needing to ask anyone's permission. Now it does need planning permission; and it also feels the need to make public its long-term intentions in advance so that local communities can be consulted and the planning authority demand whatever modifications it thinks necessary. Very often, however, reinstatement after mineral extraction tends to be for recreation rather than agriculture. The result is commendable, but not especially rural in character. One big exception is open-cast coal extraction. Here reinstatement is very carefully controlled: the cycle is three to four years coaling, reinstatement, then five years of management under Ministry of Agriculture control. Seeing once-open-cast land being farmed after that five year period, one can scarcely credit the turmoil of black mud and machinery in a hole 50 feet deep that it was before reinstatement. Thus the 36,000 acres that the Coal Board's Opencast Executive hold for coaling are, in a real sense, a borrowing only; no single acre is permanently lost to the countryside. In many cases the contrary holds true: derelict land round collieries or pockets of other superannuated industry which was lost to farming a century ago is now, in worthwhile quantities, coming back to it. Since 1942, 119,000 acres of derelict land have been restored in this way. Nonetheless, the impact of open-casting on the countryside here and now is unpleasant in scale and nature.

The electricity industry is another great urbaniser. In 1925, it generated some 5,000 million units; in 1974-5 the corresponding figure was 208,000 million—something like a 40-fold increase. Urban demand was clearly the main cause, but it is arguable that rural areas benefitted disproportionately from the ready availability of this convenient form of energy. They after all had generally never had gas. The price for the countryside was the increasing size of power stations (Bankside in the late 1940s was considered a giant with a generating capacity of about 120MW; a typical power station size today is 2,000MW). Big power stations usually meant rural sites on coast or river where cooling water was readily available in large quantities, and any pollution risk from the early nuclear stations would affect no big town. Power stations did not grow uglier as they grew bigger. Great generating halls like those at Cockenzie on the Firth of Forth and Trawsfynydd in Snowdonia have a certain excitement and grandeur to most eyes, and in certain lights may appear beautiful. But they are huge artefacts and (not at Cockenzie, but certainly at Trawsfynydd) do intrude into, and detract from, unspoiled natural landscape. They, however, are the lesser intrusion.

With them, because of their siting, came the need to run high voltage transmission lines on huge pylons long distances across unspoiled countryside where no hint of urbanisation previously showed itself. In 1961 England and Wales had 7,124 route miles of grid transmission line; by 1975 (if we include line handed over to the area boards for local distribution) the figure had risen to more than 13,800. But during the 1950s and '60s voltages had been stepped up from 132kv to 275kv and then to 400kv, with a resultant increase in pylon height from 86ft to 168ft. There are plenty of energy conservationists who would like the doctrine of Small is Beautiful to apply to electricity generation, thus reducing both dependence on the grid and the need for more and bigger transmission lines in the future. If it ever happened, that would be reversing the whole trend in the electricity industry, which provides perhaps the most vivid post-war illustration of the principle of economy of scale.

A recent (and to many people frightening) manifestation of economic growth's impact on the countryside results from the search for and exploitation of North Sea oil and gas. This is, of course, a phenomenon of the last few years only, but already it is becoming apparent that we must look at two distinct kinds of effect on rural areas. First and most obviously concern was for the coastal landscape. We should recognise that the way in which local planning authorities have insisted on early landscape and siting advice and on reinstatement, and the way in which the oil firms have engaged some of the leading landscape advisers for this purpose, represents a gain on what would have happened with any similarly sited industry 50 years ago. On the other hand, the scale of operations and of the artefacts is that much greater.

I shall never forget my first sight of the oil platform under construction at Nigg on the east coast of Scotland. The two headlands which guard the entrance to Cromarty Firth were utterly dwarfed by that North Sea monster. But, given that reinstatement takes place, such operations may be regarded as a temporary aberration. The social and psychological effect on people's lives cannot so easily be blotted out. Oil men and oil money pour in in a frenetic rush to get the job done. Their pace and style of life is totally alien to that of the countryside, and especially of the Scottish highlands. The local economy suffers severe strains and distortions as the only baker in a village goes off to seek his fortune as a well-paid labourer. No one can find a bricklayer or plumber for love nor money because oil needs their skills and will pay over the odds for them, brooking no delay and heedless of the effects on local communities.

And this brings me to a final, more general point about the effects of a growth economy on the countryside. North Sea oil is only doing to these places in a more extreme and rapid way what economic growth has done for decades to the British countryside. It is shrinking its economic value. The village shop which used to provide a living for a whole extended family is now scarcely viable even for a retired couple who pay no rent and, in effect, subsidise it with their pension. It probably sells very little local produce. The frozen vegetable firms have bought the pea crop before it was planted. The farm-worker's wife, who has seen the gap between her man's wage and the factory worker's widen, pays over the odds for a packet of frozen vegetables, or for foodstuffs which, on the old mixed farm, she would not have needed to buy. Market towns and villages, self-sufficient for centuries, have suddenly been faced with the choice posed by the GLC's overspill towns' schemes watchword: 'Expand or Die'. But expansion cannot be, as in the past, a gradual, little-by-little process.

Economics of scale forbid that, as the villagers of Blagdon in what is now Avon County discovered recently. Village opinion favoured expansion, until a Woodspring District planner pointed out the implications. The primary school would take very little increase; the sewage works was at or near its limit. To justify an extra school and extension of the sewage works, the village population would need to double, and quite rapidly at that. The villagers drew back: they perhaps sensed that this would dilute the community too much, as well as causing excessive upheaval. Blagdon in a way represents the rural dilemma. Countrymen know in their bones that, socially as well as aesthetically, Small is Beautiful. But the bread-and-butter lessons of the last five decades tell them quite the opposite: that Big pays the Bounty.

CHAPTER 13

NEWSPAPERS AND NEWSPAPERMEN

Crispin Gill

When I joined *The Western Morning News* in 1934 the paper still had advertisements filling the front page, and a double-column headline was rare. The change to front page news did not come until several years after World War II, with national news moving from the main inside news page to the front-page, two or three double-column headlines on each page as a matter of course, and the old full page of pictures replaced by more pictures mixed with the news. That pattern has been the same through the regional morning papers and the weekly papers followed suit even more slowly. Evening papers have had front-page news for most of this century but because they are printed in the afternoon and have about an hour for distribution before offices and factories finish for the day and those customers must be caught, they have always been limited in reality to the big towns.

The morning papers on the other hand start printing about midnight and have five or six hours for distribution, so they are the true country daily papers. They do serve the big provincial cities, but their circulation strength is in the countryside, where the challenge from evening papers is hardly felt and the London papers reach less efficiently, usually with only an early edition which contains less up-to-date news than the regional paper. In fact the further from London the printing centre the stronger the morning paper tends to be. It has an advantage in its compression of national and world news usually into one, more easily digested page. Because its staff live with their customers and are told very quickly if their local news is inaccurate or inadequate, they tend to be more trusted.

First radio in the 1920s and then television in the 1950s were forecast as the killers of these newspapers but they are stronger now than ever. The big stories that come over the air serve as appetisers for the papers; they have almost replaced contents bills. There has also been rationalisation; no provincial area can support two papers and the old days when every town had its Liberal and its Conservative paper are forgotten. The process began in the 1920s and accelerated in the 1930s, largely under the London competition to build up chains of local papers, daily and weekly. Many papers went to the wall then and monopoly fears led to the first Press Commission of 1948. That and the suspicions of the Socialists of all newspapers—for most provincial papers are Tory—really ended the chain-building; the only significant grouping since World War II has been that of United Newspapers. They have respected local editorial independence—as have all the surviving chains—and financially the country papers are stronger than their overstaffed and prestigious Fleet Street rivals. It is generally reputed that the provincial papers of Associated News has kept the *Daily Mail* alive for years.

The same kind of rationalisation has happened with the weeklies; it would be hard to find a town now with two papers and in many cases half a county will be served with localised editions of one paper, where each edition was once a separate paper. Some of the small ones do survive, ranging from the faintly comic to the new-fangled brassy productions often owned by newspapermen who have achieved the great dream, retired from Fleet Street and bought their own weekly. It is nearly possible from the new format to recognise the Fleet Street home of its owner. But the old-fashioned weeklies march on and they are usually the strongest in circulation and readership loyalty. The kind of reader who would not believe that World War I was over till she read it in the *West Briton* is not dead. It is the provincial papers also, weekly and daily, which have been the pioneers in leaving hot-metal printing for lithography and offset printing. They could find room and capital to build new plant on the outskirts of their towns where Fleet Street has not been able to face the capital costs of more extensive plant, or find the space.

The country papers are still the editorial training-ground for Fleet Street. As in most occupations the turn-over of staff since World War II has rapidly increased because there are jobs to be had not only on the London papers but in public relations, television and radio. I am constantly faced with Fleet Street by-lines of men from my staff, and familiar faces on the television screen.

Many good journalists stay on the country papers; it may mean less money and glamour but offers a better life. We may not have the old-time characters any more: the first man I worked with had been the Editor's secretary and told stories of picking up chorus girls from the Theatre Royal in a cab (one night the wheel came off); Martin Endle used to walk Plymouth Hoe with Cecil Rhodes while he awaited his London train; old George Smith the leader writer had covered the meetings which led to the building of the Yealmpton railway and would go out on horse-back with a basket of pigeons at the saddle bow to bring back his story. We still had the pigeon loft (and its droppings) in my first building, though the pigeons had gone, and Barny Prideaux, my stone hand and as rustic as they came, started as a boy looking after the pigeons.

Then and now the key man of any country paper was the district reporter, working away from head office, on his own and as it suited him, but staying in one district for decades. My fellow-apprentice Charlie Dean has been in Bodmin for forty years; Jim Butcher in Barnstaple nearly as long and manages to be the Agricultural Correspondent as well. He talks to ministers of the Crown as he does to the cattle auctioneer or last year's mayor; he was probably at school with the last two anyway. These men, and in small country towns the weekly paper reporter who is often correspondent of the regional paper and most of Fleet Street as well, know the countryside as well as anyone. They see the whole range of human activity; there is little that they do not know (though much they can never publish) and they are never so close as to be unable to see the wood for the trees.

Not many of us have seen the full fifty years of this survey, but we began work in the Depression that had changed little from 1927. Now the farms are looking healthy, the farmers have their cars (and some on the right soils their yachts as well). Agriculture, the mainstay of rural England, pays but at a price. To take modern machines the lanes have been widened, the hedgerow trees and often the hedges too removed. Farming is no longer the surest guarantor of the English landscape, as was thought right up to the years after the War. Farm-workers are better paid (though still not on level terms with townspeople), in better homes, with most mod cons. The country towns and villages are brighter with new paint than we have seen them; the dirt and dilapidation and flapping posters of the 1920s have gone. But half of them are ringed with de- velopers' dreadfuls, or else tarted-up to look like film sets. Planning has not kept out the toffee-box lid bow window with its little square panes, and farm buildings of any shape, size, material and monstrosity can be slapped up almost anywhere. The clever boys have found ways to lose money on farms, to set against industrial profits, or to beat tax problems with forestry; they may be coming unstuck at the time of writing but they have made their marks on the rural economy. The county agri- cultural shows, and the big national events, have settled down into fixed sites instead of moving about the countryside; it is possible to go to one of these shows now and think farming was nothing but machinery and show-jumping.

To serve the motor car the old turnpikes have been straightened and widened, given concrete kerbs and fences in place of hedges, but the quantity of travellers has revived the old roadside inns. There is a wealth of good country hotels again, and few pubs do not offer a ploughman's lunch (save the term!) or more ambitious meals. The beer has never been better looked after, although half the chemical concoc- tions are not worth caring for. If Courages sold their copper mine and all the other breweries buried their interior decorators and took all the juke boxes for a funeral pyre, the pubs would be pleasanter than in most of our lifetimes.

Village after village has lost its school and its policeman and the parson now has a group of parishes; leadership is removed but the educational standards are better, the policing probably more efficient, and the priest diligent and devoted to his flock. There are group ministries in the Anglican Church, the denominations are beginning to work to- gether and ecumenicalism is coming from the grass roots. It may be the drawing together of Christians beleaguered in a secular world but it makes for strength. Fifty years ago the last of the barn-storming theatre companies were still on the road; I saw *East Lynne* in Plympton as late as 1938. But fit-up cinemas in the smallest of country towns killed them, even as television has in turn killed these and the cinema shows touring the villages. In Tavistock the Corn Exchange with its classical façade became the cinema; now it is a supermarket. But television can be a great boon to the countryman; it has its rubbish but, more important, its educational force too.

Not just individual buildings have changed. Development companies out for the quick return have, with the cheap concession to the local authority, destroyed much of our country towns. They have moved most avidly into the towns within a hundred miles of London into which metropolitan industries have moved. Swindon was a lost market town till the Great Western made it a locomotive works and an industrial town; now the railway is just a station and the town looks a plate-glass dream from H. G. Wells.

Country doctors work more and more in partnerships based on health centres. The old respect and affection survives, and the service and the care is more efficient. If small communities fought hard enough they have kept their cottage hospitals, but they are now little more than geriatric establishments and any more serious case is moved to the general hospital up to twenty miles away. Where hospitals are not overcrowded, facilities and nursing care have improved, but it is rare to find buses still running in visiting hours.

In politics the Conservatives still hold most of rural England although the landowner's son is less often the member of Parliament. The Liberals outside the Celtic fringes are reduced to beavering handfuls of earnest people, and the Labour Party is still trying to capture the council estates. On county councils and in some district councils, party political labels have appeared but the only real difference is that the man who yesterday called himself Independent now calls himself Tory. The Magistrates' Courts have been deluged with work; motoring offences predominate but the spate of new legislation of our times has also added to their load. So the old benches of seven or eight magistrates sitting together are now split between two or three courts. The magistrates are younger and drawn from a wider spectrum of society, but the trade union justices of the cities are rare birds on country benches.

Increasingly the countryside is a place of recreation for the townsman. Commercially the canals have died but they are reviving for pleasure boats; not long-boats now but 'noddy boats' as the old men say. Country parks have had to be established to draw off the crowds from national parks. Association football is the major village sport, as it is nationally, and League ideas are creeping in. Ambitious country town clubs recruit players from the nearest city; the team bus will often start there and not from the town whose name the team bears, and after the match it is not unknown for players to find a few pounds in their boots.

But if the major, all-class recreation now is gardening, with bird-watching second, then the new middle-class sport is in the amenity movement. The old-established societies like the Dartmoor Preservation Association have become fiercely militant and every threat—gravel pits, new motorways, reservoirs, new aerodromes—has produced its own residents' association which stays in business after the immediate battle is over. The growth of these pressure groups has forced Parliament to write public participation into much new planning legislation.

To draw up a balance sheet of gains and losses in the countryside would mean matching imponderables. Many of the social changes are not just rural but national, universal in western civilisation. Half a century ago Robertson Scott was fighting basically for a basic standard of living, a better quality of life, for country people. That has been achieved, and the leavening of village life with urban-based people has been invigorating in the main. But these improvements, these new migrations, this recreational pressure, have brought new threats to peace and beauty. A dynamic landscape cannot remain unchanged; the struggle now is to ensure that the rural advance is not rural ruin, that economic improvements do not mean the unnecessary destruction of the British countryside.

FURTHER READING

CHAPTER 1
England's Green and Pleasant Land J. W. Robertson Scott (Cape 1927, Penguin 1949)
'We' and Me J. W. Robertson Scott (W. H. Allen 1956)

CHAPTER 2
Agriculture K. A. H. Murray (HMSO & Longmans, Green 1955)
British Agriculture Astor and Rowntree (Longmans, Green 1938)
Farming in Britain Today J. G. S. & Frances Donaldson (Allen Lane 1969)
Principles for British Agricultural Policy H. T. Williams (OUP 1960)
We Plough the Fields Tristram Beresford (Pelican Books 1975)

CHAPTER 3
The History of British Bus Services John Hibbs (David & Charles 1968)
The Railway Age Michael Robbins (Dufour 1962)
The Rolling Road L. A. G. Strong (Hutchinson 1956)
The Rural Transport Problem David St John Thomas (Routledge & Kegan Paul 1963)

CHAPTER 4
Country Planning R. J. Green (Manchester University Press 1971)
The Quiet Revolution Peter Ambrose (Chatto & Windus 1974)
Rural Geography Hugh D. Clout (Pergamon 1972)
The Urban Countryside R. H. Best and A. W. Rogers (Faber 1973)

CHAPTER 5
The Country and the City Raymond Williams (Chatto & Windus 1973)
The Idea of Landscape and the Sense of Place John Barrell (Cambridge University Press 1972)
Early to Rise: A Suffolk Morning Hugh Barrett (Faber 1967)
Suffolk Scene Julian Tennyson (Blackie 1939)

CHAPTER 6
The 1970s reorganisation of local government has been so recent that its history has yet to be written.

CHAPTER 7
The Englishman's Holiday A. A. R. Pimlott (Faber 1947)
Recreation in the Countryside Coppock and Duffield (Macmillan 1975)
The Seaside Sarah Howell (Collier Macmillan 1934)

Tourism Burkart and Medlik (Heinemann 1974)
Tourism, Blessing or Blight? George Young (Penguin 1973)

CHAPTER 8
The Forest and Man Robert K. Winters (Vantage Press)
Tomorrow's Countryside Garth Christian (John Murray)
Forest Service George Ryle (David & Charles)
The Forestry Commission has issued a very large number of bulletins, leaflets and guides on most aspects of their work. The *Forest Guides* of individual large forests or of well-wooded districts are especially informative. Information from the Librarian, Forestry Commission, Alice Holt, Wrecclesham, Farnham, Surrey.

CHAPTER 9
English Fox-Hunting Raymond Carr (Weidenfeld & Nicolson 1975)
Fly Fishing Tactics on Rivers Geoffrey Bucknall (Muller 1968)
Game Shooting Robert Churchill (Michael Joseph 1971)
The History of Foxhunting Roger Longrigg (Macmillan 1976)
The New Society David Holdsworth (Thames Valley Police, Kidlington, Oxford 1975)
The Wild Red Deer of Exmoor E. R. Lloyd (Exmoor Press 1975)

CHAPTER 10
Atlas of the British Flora F. H. Peering and S. M. Walters (Nelson 1962)
Breeding Birds of Britain and Ireland John Parslow (Poyser 1973)
The Changing Flora and Fauna of Britain D. L. Hawksworth (ed) (Academic Press 1974)
The Handbook of British Mammals H. N. Southern (Blackwell Scientific Publications 1964)
The Naturalist in Britain David Elliston Allen (Allen Lane 1976)
Nature Conservation in Britain L. Dudley Stamp (Collins 1969)
The Pattern of Animal Communities Charles S. Elton (Methuen 1966)
The Seabirds of Britain and Ireland Stanley Cramp, W. R. P. Bourne & David Saunders (Collins 1974)

CHAPTER 11
England and the Octopus Sir Clough Williams-Ellis (Blackie, reprinted 1975)
Future Landscapes Edited by Malcolm MacEwen (Chatto & Windus 1976)
Nature in Trust John Sheail (Blackie)
Tom Stephenson A Tribute by the Ramblers' Association on his 83rd Birthday (Ramblers' Association 1976)

CHAPTER 12
Akenfield Ronald Blythe (Penguin 1969)
The Diseconomics of Growth H. V. Hodson (Pan/Ballantine 1972)
Goodbye, Britain? Tony Aldous (Sidgwick & Jackson 1975)
Modern Agriculture and Rural Planning John Weller (Architectural Press 1967)
New Lives, New Landscapes Nan Fairbrother (Penguin 1972)
The Valley Elizabeth Clarke (Faber 1969)
Wilderness and Plenty (Reith Lectures) Frank Fraser (Ballantine 1970)

CHAPTER 13

Most books concerned with the Press concentrate on the national rather than the provincial Press, although individual newspapers have produced commemorative histories at their centenaries or similar celebrations. One exception, though again concerned with one group, is *The Men who Carry the News*, the story of United Newspapers, by Guy Schofield (Cranford Press 1975).

INDEX

Page numbers in italic indicate illustrations.